TEACHING:

A FIELD MANUAL

ADAM M GREENWOOD

Copyright © 2021 Adam M Greenwood

All rights reserved

About the author

Adam M Greenwood is the Headmaster of The Pointer School in London and is a former British Army officer. He has taught in both the state and independent sector, at Primary and Secondary level. He graduated from Loughborough University after reading Geography and went on to commission as an Army Officer after attending the Royal Military Academy Sandhurst. He saw active duty in Afghanistan with the Royal Signals and later left the Regular Army to take up a post as a Reserve Officer with the London Scottish Regiment, completing the Platoon Commanders Battle Course. He completed his PGCE at UCL IOE whilst teaching unqualified in a state school in South London. He later moved to the independent sector. He went on to complete an MBA in Educational Leadership (International) at UCL IOE in 2019, where the focus of his dissertation was middle leadership development. He became Headmaster of The Pointer School, a Prep and Pre-Prep in 2019 and started an Education EdD doctorate in 2020, focusing on Head Teacher motivation.

Teaching: A Field Manual

For Kacey, Katty, James & Matilda Ruth

Premise of the Book

There is no silver bullet to being a successful teacher – if that is what you are looking for, then you have come to the wrong place. Forget the hacks, the short cuts, and the theory that you think will save you, none of it works. What this book does offer is practical solutions to becoming a highly productive and ultimately more successful teacher.

How do you measure success in the classroom? Simple – the students are happy, and their results are good. No matter how much teachers deny it, we are in a results driven business and if the progress, SATs, GCSE and A Level results are poor, then the buck stops with you. I accept that there will always be that one particular year group, or the class from hell, but if you are producing good results year on year, then you are a success.

Many of the methods discussed in this book may seem unrealistic at first glance and somewhat over exaggerated to the casual reader. However, trust me, these are the methods that I employ every single day in my job as a teacher. Although I had the privilege of developing much of what I know at the Royal Military Academy Sandhurst and through a short military career, all the principles I suggest are simple and can be learnt and applied in your own career as a teacher. Teaching and the military are not fit for the short-term planner, they are careers for long term thinkers, planners, and leaders.

I am often asked about my role as an Army Officer and too often I hear people react with "that's a big change of career" or "teaching and the Army must be very different". Well, the simple fact is, they are not. They are actually very similar with two key factors:

1 - Leadership

2 - Discipline

In the Army we have field manuals to help us in every aspect of our profession, we carry it with us, and we use it often. If you need to know how to establish a LZ (landing zone), clear a VP (vulnerable point) or conduct orders for an advance to contact, use your field manual. This book offers the same for you, as a teacher - luckily however, the risk of death is removed!

Read this book, and then use it where you feel necessary to reference your areas of need. Keep it by your computer, or on your desk, and when you are unsure of what to do, or your workload is running away from you, pick this book back up and access everything you need.

Language used in the book

BLUF - Bottom line up front

CPD – Continuous Professional Development

DSL – Designated Safeguarding Lead

ECF – Early Career Framework

ECT – Early Career Teacher

ISI – Independent Schools Inspectorate

ITT – Initial Teacher Training

OFSTED – Office for Standards in Education

PGCE – Postgraduate Certificate in Education

Pupil/Student – These are used interchangeably, and both refer to school aged children

SLT – Senior Leadership Team

Sections

Personal skills

1	-	If you've only got a minute, it only takes a minute	14
2	-	80% solution	16
3	-	Do it nice or do it twice	18
4	-	Any fool can be uncomfortable	18
5	-	No cuff too tough	20
6	-	Army time	21
7	-	Integrity and courage	22
8	-	Confidence	23
9	-	Self-discipline	24
10	-	Professionalism	25
11	-	Selfless commitment	26
12	-	Respect for others	27
13	-	Out of your comfort zone	29
14	-	Prioritisation	30
15	-	Marginal gains	31
16	-	Decision fatigue	34
17	-	Do something your future self will thank you for	35
18	-	Dripping tap	36
19	-	Work-life balance	37
20	-	Sleep	38

Classroom skills

21	-	Lesson planning – No plan survives first contact	40
22	-	Resources	42
23	-	Subject knowledge	44
24	-	Homework	47
25	-	Planning ahead	50
26	-	AFL	51
27	-	Behaviour	53
28	-	Form tutor	61
29	-	Starters	65
30	-	Plenaries and the end of the lesson	66
31	-	Marking vs feedback	67
32	-	Questioning	69
33	-	Rewards	70
34	-	Classroom design	72
35	-	Support staff	74
36	-	Photocopying	75
37	-	Presence	76
38	-	Challenge/Differentiation	77
39	-	SEN/EAL	78
40	-	Tribal classroom	80

Professional skills

41	-	Dealing with parents	82
42	-	Parent's evening	84
43	-	Staffroom etiquette	85
44	-	Dress	86
45	-	Your attendance to school	88
46	-	Holidays	88
47	-	Commuting	90
48	-	Assemblies	91
49	-	Open days	92
50	-	Emails	93
51	-	Clubs	94
52	-	Duty	95
53	-	Trips	96
54	-	Networking	97
55	-	Socialising	98
56	-	Safeguarding	99
57	-	Dealing with stress	100
58	-	Hierarchy	102
59	-	Emotional intelligence	103
60	-	Know your school and its surroundings	105

Your career

61	-	Picking the right school	106
62	-	State vs Independent vs Grammar	108
63	-	Primary vs Secondary	112
64	-	Interviews	113
65	-	Salary	118
66	-	ECT years (formerly known as the NQT year)	120
67	-	Making your life easier	122
68	-	Annual Review	123
69	-	Teaching Unions	125
70	-	Doing CPD	126
71	-	Leading CPD	127
72	-	Doing a Masters	128
73	-	Doing a Doctorate	129
74	-	Middle Leadership	130
75	-	Pastoral Roles	132
76	-	Academic Roles	133
77	-	SLT	134
78	-	Governorship	136
79	-	PGCE/ITT Applications	137
80	-	PGCE/ITT Interviews	139

Leadership

81	-	Either lead, follow or get out of the way	142
82	-	Core Leadership	143
83	-	Service test	144
84	-	7 Questions	84
85	-	Oodaloop	154
86	-	SOPs	155
87	-	Seek early victories	157
88	-	Leadership is lonely	159
89	-	Inspection	160
90	-	Extreme ownership	161
91	-	There are no casual conversations	163
92	-	Never say yes in the corridor	164
93	-	Coaching/mentoring	165
94	-	Command and control at all levels	166
95	-	Slow leadership - condor moment	167
96	-	The standard you walk past is the standard you accept	168
97	-	Get comfortable with being uncomfortable	170
98	-	The power of habits	171
99	-	Is this the hill you want to die on?	172
100	-	Headship	173

Teaching: A Field Manual

Section 1 - Personal Skills

"

Moral courage is higher and a rarer virtue than physical courage.

"

Field Marshal General Slim

1 - If you've only got a minute, it only takes a minute

BLUF - Many tasks in teaching can take an almost unlimited amount of time. Set yourself a time limit for every task, timetable in when you are going to complete it, and stick to it.

This is one of the core philosophies in the Army that I live by in teaching, and indeed every aspect of my life. If you've only got a minute, it only takes a minute. Many tasks in teaching have an almost unlimited capacity for how long they can take to complete. Teaching also has several tasks going on at once that all need managing. You may find that you have four classes worth of books to mark, six lessons to plan to teach alongside a parents' evening, end of terms tests, and administration for your form group. To complete all these tasks successfully you need to set yourself dedicated time limits of how long you are willing to or can afford to spend on each task. If you take in a stack of thirty-four books, when are you going to mark them and how long is that going to take? Well, if you sit down with the view of marking them in the evening, then you are already destroying your work-life balance. Ultimately, you will procrastinate on other tasks and spend the whole evening unproductively marking, only to have your pupils spend approximately ten seconds looking at the feedback you have provided.

If you've only got a minute, it only takes a minute. Take in the books, timetable in when you are going to mark them and set yourself a rigid time structure to achieve this. If you take on board the recommendations in the marking and feedback sections, thirty-four books should take you no more than thirty minutes to get through. There is only so much value that you are going to add with marking and feedback. Instead, you can do more valuable things with your time - do not spend hours and hours on books, it is not sustainable when you could be teaching ten plus classes a week. Once you have allocated yourself a specific time to achieve each task, set a timer and cut yourself away from all distractions, that includes your phone and emails. If you need to leave your regular workspace to achieve this, go to a quiet area of the library and avoid any distractions. If you find it difficult to stick to the thirty minute limit at first, get a 'Tabata timer' on your phone and set yourself a limit per book and work at it.

You must be disciplined with your time if you are realistically going to achieve everything you need to and still have a life. You should not be working more than fifty hours per week as a teacher. This will not include additional commitments such as parents' evenings and running a sports team on a Saturday but should be used as a rough guide of how much you work per week, if you are to sustain in the profession. Divide up your week and this will allow you to analyse your time available. If you are in school from 0800-1700 each day then you will need to add up your prescribed tasks, such as: lessons, form time, duty, and time for a lunch and morning break. Then, distribute your remaining time as available; for example, if you are on a full teaching timetable with a form group and no additional responsibilities, you may find that you have less than fifteen hours per week to complete all the other required tasks in a given week.

Plan, stick to it, and use the time effectively.

2 - 80% solution

BLUF: Do not over plan your lessons. Add value where you can and plan to 80%. Allow your teaching skills, subject knowledge, and the learners in front of you to guide the other 20%.

Teaching is not a profession for perfectionists. There are many aspects of the job that are never finished, and an avid perfectionist will find themselves constantly in a deep hole. If you are a perfectionist, or have tendencies to be, and you are already a teacher, it is time to change some of your focuses to an 80% solution.

One of the biggest mistakes I see teachers doing is over planning. When you first start teaching, lesson planning will take you far longer than the value it adds. Naturally, when you first start planning you have little idea of how to put a lesson together. We have all sat through thousands of hours of lessons when we were at school, but probably never gave any thought about their design as an adolescent. Looking back, it is hard to remember these lessons from your younger years and the classroom environment probably looks somewhat different.

The Army is known for its level of precision and planning but unlike much of popular belief, everything is not planned down to a tee. In fact, many Officers and Soldiers plan to an 80% solution, I have taken this philosophy through all my lesson planning and it saves me hours.

Every classroom has a plethora of uncontrollable factors when teaching any subject. What do the pupils already know? What questions will they ask? How long will the tasks take them? Will they fully grasp the concepts? Are the class behaving? The list can go on and on. There is no reason to plan a lesson to total perfection. If you can plan your lesson to about 80% of what you plan to cover and get them to do, this will suffice. The other 20% will be designed from your on the spot reactions to questions, how the learning is developing, and your ability to add value and impact to the topic.

Some of the best lessons I have ever taught have been lessons that have not been over planned and tied to a PowerPoint. Instead, they are free flowing in the direction of the learners in the classroom. It can often be more harmful to pupil learning if you stick to a lesson plan than if you allow flexibility and creativity as directed by the classroom. The best way to see this in action is to teach two classes from the same year group, the same lesson and to see how the lesson evolves. Although you should absolutely stay on the path of getting from A to B, how you get there may vary dramatically, and this will be positive for all learners.

I have seen teachers go to the extreme of planning everything from the questions that they will ask at various points of the lesson to writing down everything they plan to say. This is not only ineffective and something you should be able to address comfortably from fine-tuning your profession but is also not sustainable when you come to teaching a full timetable. When on a busy timetable you need to add value where you can and save time in every way possible, the 80% solution allows you to do this and as you become a more seasoned teacher you may be able to plan to a 70% or 60% solution in quick time.

3 - Do it nice or do it twice

BLUF: If you poorly complete a task you will have to do it again.

A classic at Sandhurst. Our Colour Sargant would bark at us as we were polishing our shoes, "do it nice or do it twice". The same as we prepared for room inspections, ironed our uniform, or completed a fitness test.

When completing tasks, you will find yourself doing it again if you do not properly and execute it the first time around. This is not to say that after doing something you cannot evaluate and improve it, but there is a limit of acceptability. When planning lessons, we all know the lesson that you plan over a longer period of time and the children get a lot out of it. At the same time, we all know the lesson that is a quick introduction question followed by a video and some textbook work.

Investing the right amount of time the first time round will not only ensure a better outcome for the pupils, but also a better outcome for you as the teacher. If you poorly mark the children's work the first time around, they might not grasp the concepts and improvements required, leading to more misconceptions and a second teaching of the subject area. "Do it nice or do it twice".

4 - Any fool can be uncomfortable

BLUF: There is no pride to be taken in working all the hours God sends - take care of yourself.

In the Infantry we would go on field exercises regularly, this more often than not was in Wales or over in another place with inordinate amounts of rain. You do not realise how much it rains in the UK until you are outside for weeks at a time. The idea of any fool being uncomfortable is that any fool can stand in the rain and suffer rather than put on an extra layer of warm kit and waterproofs. Any fool can have wrecked feet for failing to administer their feet properly with dry socks and powder. Any fool can be hungry because they did not eat enough.

In teaching, there is, in many schools, a culture of suffering. A culture of being in work very early and leaving very late, working into the early hours of the morning lesson planning, and spending your weekends marking essays and books. Do not become this person, there is no gain to be had working yourself into the ground. Take pride in your own self-care, ensuring you can eat a healthy lunch, still work out each day and get to bed at a good time. Back to the concept of "if you've only got a minute, it only takes a minute", you must put boundaries in place to safeguard yourself and ensure the pupils have a well-rested and refreshed teacher in front of them each day. "Any fool can be uncomfortable."

One of the most useful pieces of advice I ever received in teaching came at my second school. I was at a new staff induction meeting along with all the other new teachers to the school. At this particular meeting, the Headmaster was there to give his words of guidance to be effective in the school. Here he said that:

> "I do not want to see you running around the corridors, stressed at a hundred miles per hour, if I do that is when I will be concerned. A good teacher who has got everything together can sit in the staffroom at breaktime, confident in the knowledge that their work is at hand and a cup of coffee and a break will allow them to be more productive for the rest of the day."

I have taken this quite literally and I am a better professional for it. This will allow you to avoid burn out and remain at the top of your game for longer. People joining the profession in their early twenties could find themselves in the classroom for over forty years with today's rising pensionable age. Think about what is sustainable for you over weeks, months, terms, and years.

5 – "No cuff too tough"

BLUF: No one really has it all together, so cuff it until you have some idea of what you are doing.

"No cuff too tough" is the Army's take on doing something, literally without any preparation. Now, this is not something to promote as a daily practice, but we are all going to find ourselves in positions where we do not feel we are capable of doing what is asked of us. As a cadet at Sandhurst, many spend the majority of the forty-four weeks of training thinking they are a few inches away from being thrown out for not being capable enough. Over time, we realised there was "no cuff too tough" and we must simply have the confidence to pull things together until we actually could. This has not changed in the classroom, unqualified, feeling like I had no hope of teaching lessons that would progress children's learning. However, what I found was that with a "no cuff too tough" approach I could enter the classroom and look like a teacher, act like a teacher and eventually be a very good one.

Even as a Headmaster and parent today I find myself in positions where I do not truly know what I am doing, and I find myself having to cuff it. This does not mean you make it up, but what it does mean is that you can think fast on your feet and develop into the individual and professional that you want to be.

6 - Army time

BLUF: If you are not five minutes early, you are late.

Being on time is a big deal in the military. Many a film has depicted a soldier getting a real telling off for being late to parade. The simple reason behind this is that if you do not have timeliness embedded into the core of your being, you will be late and make a mistake on timings; doing so is mission-critical and could cost lives. In military planning, H-Hour denotes the start of a mission and could start with an airstrike or movement to a location. Being even seconds late can compromise the whole mission and costs lives. This is why, through training and working in the Army, it is drilled into you that if you are not five minutes early, you are late. We have all been at a meeting due to start at, let's say, 1000, and people are still rolling in two, three, five minutes after the start time. A 1000 start means the meeting starts at 1000 and you need to be there five minutes before, ready to get set up, and start the meeting on time.

Schools run to a timetable and are on par with the military in terms of the importance of timeliness. If you let your class out late, this eats into the time of the next teacher's class, this is you saying that you do not care about the start of their lesson. With meetings, turning up late shows professional incompetence and a lack of ability to make even the most basic deadlines - this will not go unnoticed by your peers and superiors.

I struggle to see how a teacher can get through the working day without a watch. Seriously, invest in any type of watch - most people in the Army wear Casio Watches that cost less than £10 but are all but indestructible. Turn up to meetings on time, finish your lessons on time, and get in control of your schedule.

7 - Integrity and courage

BLUF: Do what is right, even when no one is looking.

Teaching is one of the careers in life where your integrity is an essential part of your character and people's perception of you. Like professions such as doctors, priests, Army officers and the police, you need to keep your moral compass pointing firmly north. Make sure your social media is locked down and never write anything you would not want to see on the front page of a newspaper. Similarly, treat every email as open - you never know who will pass it on. Therefore, having integrity is key because you are automatically positioned to make the right decisions. If you let your integrity slip, it becomes easier and easier for it to slip more and more - that is why you must get off on the right foot from the very start.

Courage, similar to integrity, is something you have to have from the start and the more you let it slip, the more it will slip. Have the courage to tell a pupil that their behaviour is not acceptable, or that their shirt is not tucked in. If a teacher is not marking their books or their lessons are not up to scratch, let them know. You must have the courage to do these things, or you become a bystander in the very school you are giving your life to work in. Remember, the standard you walk past is the standard you accept. If you do not want your students to litter, pick a piece of litter up as you walk past it. If you want a tidy classroom, keep your desk tidy. People will notice and people will follow your lead. Never forget the level of influence you can have.

8 - Confidence

BLUF: Whether you think you have it or not, you must have a high level of confidence to have put yourself in the classroom.

Many of the best teachers have a far more calm and collective approach to the profession. In the same way, some of the best soldiers and officers (many of which joining the teaching profession) have a calm and quiet confidence in themselves.

The only way you will gain confidence is by putting yourself in positions to build it. Of course, this starts every day in the classroom when you are standing in front of a group of students who want to learn from you. However, you need to take this further to build your confidence as an educator. Perhaps the greatest arena to build this is in assemblies. Many a teacher knows the feeling of walking up on stage in front of hundreds of students, in silence, waiting for you to speak. For most, jumping straight in at the deep end is a lot to ask, but this is a skill, and a level of confidence that can be developed over time. I would advise you to start with a year group or Key Stage assembly in front of approximately one hundred students. Once you have led one or two of these your confidence will build, as will your ability to control your nerves and fears. You will be able to build up to large speaking engagements like whole school assemblies and whole staff CDP sessions. The confidence you build in these areas will transfer into the classroom where you will find that you can deal with that tricky class, that little bit better. Or, you find that more staff in the school know you from your assembly, so are willing to help you out or network with you.

The confidence you build in teaching is not something that should be underestimated. If you keep pushing yourself, it will last a lifetime, and you will be a better professional for it.

9 - Self-Discipline

BLUF: You must be disciplined to succeed in a job with a never-ending to-do list.

Discipline is at the centre of the Army. This does not mean a large Regimental Sergeant Major standing in front of a recruit with a stick and shouting, but this means having self-discipline. This is seen in all aspects of Army life, from having glass polished boots to a well-ironed uniform and smart haircut. The reason for this high level of standard is so that when the crunch moment comes, when you are going out on the ground on operations, you do not forget anything that could cost you your life. Although teaching is rarely a life-or-death situation (although some rather adventurous schools' trips have led to this), a high level of self-discipline is required to survive and thrive in the job.

One of the most memorable pieces of advice I have heard was at a CPD session. Here, the member of staff leading the session said, "I do my marking for that day before leaving because I do not want to do it today, but I won't want to do it tomorrow either." This encapsulates the fact that you need to have the self-discipline to get the tasks done. Few teachers enjoy marking but appreciate that if you do not get it done, it will just build and build and build. You *must* get it done, even if you do not want to.

This can be applied to almost any aspect of teaching - there will always be areas you enjoy more than others, but it is about having the self-discipline to get them all done, whether that be planning lessons of writing reports. One of the reasons that teachers feel overworked and do not believe the job is sustainable is due to a lack of self-discipline, which as a result, causes three things to happen:

a) The to-do list never ends

b) The tasks just build and build

c) You work extreme hours

Just like with the principle of *"if you only have a minute, it only takes a minute"* you must be disciplined with your time to ensure you do not work every evening and weekend, in order to sustain a healthy work-life balance. The to-do list in teaching will never end if you let it be that way. There is always another lesson to perfect or more marking that could have been done, you have to have the self-discipline to have a cut-off, just like you need the self-discipline to get the task done.

10 - Professionalism

BLUF: Teaching is a vocation, so you are always on duty

How many times do you see headlines in the newspaper, soldier does X, teacher does X, policeman does X. In some professions, your character and moral fibre are inexplicably linked to your job and a certain level of expectation comes with that. We are told as Army Officers that you need to be whiter than white. By this we mean that no one should have anything negative on your character, you need to have the integrity to do the right thing, even when no one is looking. As a result, people will then have confidence in you as an individual.

Professionalism also means being competent in your job. Gone are the days of being the talented amateur who could get by in their teaching career with a good university degree. The Education Reform Act in 1989 changed all of that with the introduction of inspections, making teachers far more accountable. Gone are the days of teachers sat reading the newspaper while a class copied from a textbook. It is a teacher's professional responsibility to improve their practice. This starts with subject knowledge, often developed at university but needs to be extended further. For example, as a Geography teacher you may have a great depth of knowledge about rivers, but this could be too deep for a 14 year old pupil to understand. At the same time, I had gone through my GCSE, A-Level, and Bachelor's degree in Geography without ever really learning about weather, and suddenly it is on the GCSE specification. You need to learn and read. This also goes for any exam specifications you are teaching - you need to know them inside out. Are you teaching the right thing? Is it relevant?

You also have a responsibility to improve your pedagogy, to develop your practice in the classroom, to stay up to date with the latest research and developments whilst not falling into the trap of following fads. The final part of your professional journey is to study leadership theory. Everyone is a leader, even if you are just leading yourself. You need to understand some of the different principles that leaders lead through. Look at both good and bad examples and model parts of your leadership on individuals you can relate to. These people could be people you work with, or figures from history.

11 - Selfless commitment

BLUF: No one joins teaching for the money, it's about selfless commitment to the cause.

Selfless commitment is a core aspect of the Army, you are putting yourself in harm's way for the good of others. Teaching is driven by the selfless commitment of teachers; in that you are accepting less pay and more stress for the benefit of teaching the great minds of the future. Most teachers could earn more money in another career.

Most teachers could have far less stress in another career. In fact, the suggestion is that only social workers have a more stressful job than teachers.

This is why teaching is a job of selfless commitment, you are selflessly going into the classroom to teach. You are fed by those moments of a child understanding a concept you have taught them or feeling safer for having you as a teacher. You should be proud to be a teacher, it is a career for those who want to make the world a better place.

12 - Respect for others

BLUF: Teaching will bring you close to a wide range of people, respect them all.

Schools are amazing microcosms of society. You have people from a wide array of backgrounds, doing a wide array of jobs. In schools, the teachers are just the tip of the iceberg of any academic environment. Beneath this, are a number of different support staff ensuring that teachers can operate smoothly on a day-to-day basis.

Everyone deserves respect at all levels of a school or organisation; without all of the cogs turning in the school, the wheels will come off. Imagine if the school was not cleaned for one day, one week, or even one month! Or if there was no one there on Reception to manage pupil lateness and queries. Schools simply would not function.

The same is true for the pupils. The diversity of your pupil body will ultimately depend upon the school you work in. However, even in some of the top independent schools in the UK, you have a vast range of backgrounds and wealth with many schools now offering large bursaries and support to families. Pupils will know if you like them or not, you can try your best to hide it but ultimately when you are spending hours per week with perceptive young people, they will soon catch on. You need to find the job and talent in each pupil, that is your role as a teacher and an education professional.

Many things will affect your pupils' respect for themselves and their peers; this could be socio-economic background, or a whole raft of things from friendship to body image issues. They need their teacher to respect them, and this respect and relationship will allow the pupils to learn and be successful in your classroom. Everyone has been to school, so we can all think back to a specific teacher that respected and developed our own growth.

Teaching is far more complex than being paid to teach lessons and mark books - an approach on this level in education is never successful, or indeed fulfilling. You must choose to have respect for others, it is not something you can decide not to do. Simple things like apologising to pupils or admitting your mistakes will help you, it is not a sign of weakness, it is a sign of strength of character and respect.

Teaching can be an emotional job, working with people is an emotional investment. The students need to learn, as well as be nurtured, this is a challenge and something that only those who put themselves in the classroom understands. The Army has high standards across the organisation and education, and in some areas, lacks those high standards. When I joined teaching, I stayed committed to maintaining the high standards required - pupils respect that, and in time they believe in the standard and rise to it. I would always start by telling my GCSE class they will all get A*s – of course, they did not, but the results were high. I am sure they were much better than they would have been if my respect for the classes intellectual capacity had been at the base level.

If you respect the pupils, they will, in turn, respect you.

13 - Out of your comfort zone

BLUF: A lot of teaching is out of your comfort zone, practice it!

Teaching is a career that presents situation after situation that is out of your comfort zone. In the Army, we talk about getting comfortable at being uncomfortable. The more you find yourself in the uncomfortable situations, the more you will be comfortable with it, but you must take that first step into it. Lots of teacher training is built around getting you to at least a starting point to be effective in the classroom, but to become truly comfortable, you *need* to push yourself.

Assemblies are a situation outside of most people's comfort zone and leading assemblies will build your confidence. However, being out of your comfort zone can affect many aspects of your profession.

How comfortable are you with confronting a pupil's behaviour? What if that pupil is six foot two inches, eighteen years old, and aggressive? What about the parent who you know is difficult and is happy to shout at you in front of others? If you do not get out of your comfort zone and confront these issues head-on you will never become comfortable with them, and slowly but surely your standards will slip along with your ability to do your job and your self-worth. Get comfortable with being uncomfortable. This does not mean being heartless or cruel, but it does mean standing up for what you believe in and what is right.

14 - Prioritisation

BLUF: You can live and die by your to-do list but ask yourself, does it really need to be on there?

You are hard pushed to find a teacher without some form of to-do list structure in place, whether it is in the back of a notebook, online, or some other wonderful structure. The key to the teaching to-do list is that it will never end if you let it be that way. It is essential that you can prioritise what needs to be achieved or not.

The school week has a regimented structure to it; periods, timetables, days etc. When you are planning your priorities, you need to plan around this. If you set a class a large piece of work to do for homework, when are you going to take it in? When are you going to mark it? When are you going to give it back to them? If you do not have these three things in place the wheels will fall off your prioritisation system and you will end up reacting to what needs to be done. "Oh no, I have a lesson to plan for tomorrow", or "I have a piece of homework to give back period six". You need to prioritise your to-do list.

When adding anything to your to-do list you need to ask yourself if that actually *needs* to go on your to-do list? As a rule of thumb, only add a new task to another day's schedule, rather than that day, unless it is critical e.g., a safeguarding matter.
Keep your to-do list in check, is what you have on there a 'nice to have' or an 'essential' piece of work? Does that literacy mat need making today, or could it wait for a quieter period? Could you ask someone else to make it? Has someone already made it? With careful management around your priorities, you can ensure your to-do list stays manageable.

15 - Marginal gains

BLUF: Time is vital in teaching, make gains in every possible area.

In the Army, you will often have a very full schedule. At Sandhurst, the day is deliberately made to be jam-packed full of activities and lessons so that when you do eventually get some time back, you realise how much you can achieve in that frame.

Teaching, in a similar fashion, has very full days and if you are not careful, you can find yourself working all the hours that God sends. All whilst trying to complete a to-do list which in reality can always have more on it.

To be effective you need as much time as possible. You are unlikely to be able to save huge chunks of time in any one area, that is where marginal gains come in. You must seek to save a little time in every area. Sure, you could save six hours a week if you stopped marking your students' work, but that is not a marginal gain, that is a failure in your job role. Marginal gains will allow you to shave seconds and minutes off tasks, which across the year will save you hours and hours. Who wouldn't want to save a whole day, or more in time by implementing some simple strategies?

Here are some of my key time savers:

a) **Emails and signature preloaded -** Think about how many emails you send per day. If you are writing 'kind regards', or similar, followed by your name each time you will waste a huge amount of time. Five seconds per email, twenty emails per day, one hundred emails per week, four hundred emails per month…it goes on and on.

b) **Preloaded reply groups** – How often do you email the same groups of people? Create email groups to save you typing in the address (even if it is quick links) to the addresses and then in one click, you can email all those people.

c) **Templates** – Most of your lessons are going to have a relatively similar format if you are using PowerPoint slides or similar. Do not waste time writing in the subheadings and formatting fonts and colours, have it all in a template ready to go. The same is very useful if you write lots of letters to parents or make worksheets. Templates will save time.

d) **Buy or download lessons** - It is amazing how much reinventing of the wheel goes on in teaching. Sometimes making your own lessons is great but across the country, thousands of teachers are all creating lessons for the same exam specification or the same part of the National Curriculum. I understand that you need to personalise different aspects to your classes, but some things are universal. Download lessons for free, share with friends from other schools, or buy resources (often high quality and just about ready to go) to save yourself hours per week in lesson planning.

e) **Get your lessons planned** – There is nothing worse than starting a week without any or few lessons planned. Get your lessons in place at least a half-term in advance (a year if you can) and then you can make small tweaks along the way rather than having to produce things from scratch week-on-week or term-on-term.

f) **Routines** – How long does it take you to hand sticks of glue out? How long does it take you to hand worksheets out? To get pupils to enter the classroom and sit down? In the first few lessons with a new class, drill routines. Getting these routines right at the start will save you huge amounts of time across the year. Think about the layout of your classroom and then put drills in place. Glue drill, hand to one pupil and they then pass along the row and up. Glue back in - the same in reverse. Handing in books - in the green box as you leave the classroom by the door. Make your class practice these. Time them, and then make them do it again until they can get their time down. Pupils love a bit of competition; you will be surprised by the time you save.

g) **Learn the IT** – How often have you seen a teacher at an interactive board with no idea how to use it? Spend an hour getting to grips with the technology, and you will unlock the wealth of tools it has that your school is probably paying a small fortune for. How often does the photocopier jam? Learn some basic unjamming methods and how to change the staples - this will take you five minutes to learn but save you inordinate amounts of frustration and time in the future.

h) **Lunch** – Do not waste time making lunch each morning - either eat the school food or get a rotation in place where you make everything at the start of the week, or rollover leftovers from dinner.

i) **Breakfast** – Do not start your day off getting decision fatigue - have the same weekday breakfast and have it ready in the kitchen for when you wake up.

j) **Dress -** Do not overthink how you dress for school. Get a system in place that is quick and easy. You could have five shirts, five days, with five ties - it saves you having to think about what to wear (note: in military fashion I do not condone saving time by not ironing shirts and polishing shoes).

16 - Decision fatigue

BLUF: You will be confronted with thousands of decisions per day, take it one step at a time and avoid decision fatigue.

Do you ever feel decision fatigue? Theories suggest that there are only so many decisions you can make in a day before you become fatigued and making decisions becomes difficult. Have you ever got to the end of the school day and even deciding what to eat or watch on TV seems exhausting? As a teacher, you will have to make thousands of decisions per day due to the hundreds, or thousands of interactions you have with different people. If you are teaching a six period day with maximum class sizes, you could interact with over two hundred people before factoring in form time, after school clubs, and interactions with colleagues.

The first step to avoiding decision fatigue is to cut out the fat from your day. Have a plan of what you are going to wear in advance (X shirt and X tie or X dress etc.). Have your breakfast, lunch, and dinner planned in advance. Tiring decisions are taken out of the way which will free up parts of your brain for the day.

In school, you will have a lot of decisions to make so the more you have planned, the more you can avoid decision fatigue. You should know what out of class time you are going to have in advance - how are you going to use it? Plan the marking and plan your free periods. Plan homework in advance and have the lessons ready. Although teaching does require flexibility around lessons, for concepts not understood or content not covered, generally you should be able to map your lessons out well in advance. In my first school, I remember my teaching mentor (the Deputy Head), who upon reflection was quite frankly useless at his job, telling me he generally had his lessons planned two or three in advance of the actual lesson. On arrival at this school, I joined a department with no lessons planned and a process of planning week on week. It was a total nightmare and led to a phenomenal level of decision fatigue as I negotiated teaching two Year 7 classes, two Year 8 classes, two Year 9 classes, and two GCSE classes, as an unqualified teacher. Contrast this with joining my second school where they had lessons for every year group (Year 7 to A-Level), planned and mapped out in advance with a two-year projection. This allowed a phenomenal amount of breathing space, and although lessons had to be adapted to classes and the learning that took place, the plan and the lessons were there.

You will face decision fatigue, but you can plan to manage and even avoid it if you are affectively planned and ready for the day, term, year, and beyond.

17 - Do something your future self will thank you for

BLUF: It is easy to not do something, but your future self will not thank you.

As an Army officer, one of the most difficult periods of your initial training at the Royal Military Academy Sandhurst is weeks one to five. Every minute of your waking hours are occupied, and you are lucky to get five hours sleep per night. It has to be experienced to be believed - the whole five weeks are hectic. If you decide to pause for ten minutes, you compromise your future self and crucially your ability to sleep at a future date.
Teachers face huge pressures on their time. Every day you need to do something that your future self will thank you for. Decide not to mark those books? Your future self will have to mark them, and you will have even less time than you do right now. Spontaneously set homework without giving due consideration to the task and when you are going to mark it? Your future self will have to mark this, alongside the other

homework you did not properly plan for and all of a sudden you have a mountain of marking – if you put it off, then your future self will suffer more.

My first school used to plan their topics half term by half term. This created the first complexity of topics all being different in length based on whether the term was five weeks, six weeks, or seven weeks. The other issue here was that you had the end of half term tests for all five-year groups in the same week, leading to a mountain of marking. Whereas, my second school staggered its topics so that pressure points for marking did not occur.

Do something your future self will thank you for and your life will be far easier.

18 - Dripping Tap

BLUF: Once the tap starts dripping it is hard to make it stop.

In the Army, people talk about dripping taps. This links to teaching in more ways than one. Similar to the idea of "no cuff too tough", you are going to have to get to grips with your outward persona. When you first join a school, people will be making assessments on your ability and competence as a teacher. If you do not get this right from the start, you will find it much harder further down the line to change this. We all know the strict teacher, the lazy teacher, the organised teacher, and the disorganised teacher. You need to ensure that people have the right perception of you. This comes through some basic skills:

a) Carry a notebook or a tablet.

b) Walk with purpose.

c) Dress smart - It is better to be over dressed than under dressed.

d) Be very organised - turn up to meetings early and get all your work done in advance of deadlines.

So, this takes me back to the "dripping tap" analogy. If you are perceived as being rubbish at something, you are late, your books are not marked, or your reports are not uploaded then the water starts to drip, and it is really hard to stop it, so do not let it start!

19 - Work-life balance

BLUF: Work-life balance is critical to your long-term success in the profession.

Teachers, like all professionals, need a work-life balance to be effective. This habit must be instilled early in your career or the bad habits are difficult to break. If you start your career working every Saturday, that will become a habit and you will find it really hard to get out of it. You have to make a commitment when you join teaching to only work on the weekend if it is absolutely critical. This normally comes around twice per year at report writing time, but rarely, if ever, at any other points. Even in your training year, you must commit to not working on the weekend. This will allow you to have a clear perspective on the time you have available in the week and work to ensure your tasks are done within the time frame available. Do not let work consume every aspect of your life. Have downtime from emails and communication with staff. If you can avoid staff having your phone number, do! The best practice in most cases is to get all your work done in the school building so that when you leave you know your work is done. Marking at home is miserable.

If you struggle with this at first, commit certain nights of the week that you will not work. Wednesdays always work well as motivation at the start of the week, and it will help you over the mid-week hump. Lots of your ability to not work in the evening will come down to how effectively you have planned your week. Have you ensured the hand-in dates for homework are spread out enough so you do not have an incoming tsunami, or have you ended up with everything on the same night so that after a couple of days of not marking you are now in a monsoon of it? Any fool can be uncomfortable and if you are to endure as a teacher you must find a sustainable balance. You cannot work until 2200 every evening of the year; you will burn out, you need a life, what if you have your own kids? Start with the right habits early. At Sandhurst everyone is put through an intensive week 1-5 training regime to get the best habits in place, you could create your own weeks 1-5 to build your habits in teaching.

20 - Sleep

BLUF: You need sleep! Get to bed early, get up early, feel ready for the day.

So many teachers sacrifice their level of sleep in their early teaching years in an attempt to keep on top of their workload. As already suggested, you should not work into the evenings or weekends, apart from exceptional circumstances. You cannot effectively operate in the classroom without a good night's sleep. Many things will stand in the way of good sleep; your phone, marking, TV – you must avoid them all! Just like you set an alarm to wake up, you should set an alarm to go to sleep. As part of a healthy routine to be set for the day of teaching, you should go to bed at around 2130-2200 and get yourself up nice and early for a workout and breakfast. Getting up at 0530 to workout (this is also a good time to think over the day and make any decisions without distractions) and then have an hour at home for breakfast and family time before heading into school. Many teachers find it hard to sleep at night with so many tasks flying around their head - if this is you, sleep with a notebook by your bed instead of your phone, use it to take note of what springs to mind on your to-do list.

A rested mind will be more able to think, plan, make decisions and effectively teach. Especially in the latter part of long school terms, you are going to need to rest if you are to keep at the top of your game. There is no point wearing yourself out and becoming ineffective.

Teaching is very demanding through term time; it is a career of waves and troughs. The term is very intense, followed by huge dips when the end of term comes and the weeks of break. If you do not take care of yourself and make sure get enough sleep, you will not make it to the end of term in a fit state. One of two things will happen; either your performance will drop (which is no good for the pupils), or you will end up ill or burnt out and have to take time off (this is no good for your colleagues or your pupils). Manage yourself appropriately - it is a marathon, not a sprint, and any fool can be uncomfortable.

Section 2 - Classroom Skills

"

I have nothing to offer but blood, toil, tears and sweat

"

Winston Churchill

21 - Lesson planning – No plan survives first contact

BLUF: You can spend forever planning a lesson to be perfect - remember the 80% solution.

Planning lessons and teaching is not rocket science. Even planning a whole curriculum is relatively straight forward. You have a range of starters followed by a giving of information and a number of tasks to:

a) Represent this knowledge

b) Confirm understanding

The issue comes with the human factor - there is an unlimited number of variables that can happen. Although you cannot actively plan for this you can do two things:

a) Have excellent subject knowledge

b) Have strong relationships with your pupils

The key here is to remember two things; the 80% solution, and the idea that "no plan survives first contact". What this means is, you can spend hours and hours planning a lesson, from detailing every part of the learning, the questions, and even how the children will move in the classroom. You name it - but when you have first contact with the children, this can be derailed instantly.

For example, your pupils do not understand the task you have set, or some pupils are missing so your 'think pair share' task has odd numbers - the list of variables is endless. This is why, just like in the Army, no plan survives first contact and therefore needs to be adaptable. You as a teacher need to become better at responding to this, and most importantly anticipating the issues that may arise. If you know that some pupils struggle to draw pie charts, make them a template to support them. What you are doing is anticipating the situation, rather than reacting in the lesson and consequently losing valuable minutes.

This is why an 80% solution will work 95% of the time. If you have 80% of the lesson in place and planned, the other factor (the 20% variable) will come into place when the human factor comes into play. To plan a 100% solution will take you hours to plan, whereas an 80% solution might take you minutes.

In order to be productive and successful in teaching you need to accept that a great teacher is someone who produces good lessons almost all of the time. Removing the idea that all your lessons need to be perfect, outstanding lessons is key – it is simply not time possible for any teacher and would require endless amounts of planning time. Instead, choose one lesson per week for each of your classes where you will try something different, i.e., an activity you heard worked well for one of your colleagues or something you read in a teaching book. Doing this will not only allow you to develop your teaching practice, but also ensure your students are motivated and engaged in their learning through new and inspiring activities each week. Therefore, making sure all of your lessons are valuable to your students is pivotal for ensuring academic success. However, realising not all of your lessons need to be outstanding for your students to achieve this is incredibly important and will save you both time and pressure.

Finally, always start with the end in mind. What do you want to achieve in this lesson? What do you want your students to know by the end of your lesson? What are the learning objectives/outcomes? Start with the end goal and then work backwards. Planning a lesson around several specific tasks that have no relevance to the learning objectives is unproductive and detrimental to your students' success. Making sure all of your tasks contribute to the overall aim of your lesson is crucial to ensuring effective learning outcomes. The same is true here for planning an entire unit of work - start with the end in mind, i.e., start with the end of unit assessment first, not the first lesson.

22 - Resources

BLUF: Do not waste hours and hours reinventing the wheel when there are already resources out there for your subject. Buy the resources and adapt them to your specific needs.

I am constantly amazed at how many teachers across the country are constantly reinventing the wheel with the creation of resources. The number of teachers creating the same resources in their subject is staggering. What is even more amazing is when teachers in the same department are not even sharing their resources. This is a total waste of everyone's time and will consume huge chunks of your already limited time. When you first start teaching, you will find that it will take you at least an hour to produce a good one hour lesson, and at the extreme end, some teachers take three to four hours to produce a lesson (which is insane). Once you have been teaching a year or so, you should be able to get down to planning a core lesson in around ten minutes.

So, what is the solution to the resource planning problem that has taken over education? Buy some of your resources! TES has vastly improved the quality and detail of lessons on their site since it became a paid model, and other sites such as 'TeachersPayTeachers' and 'TeachIt' offer a wide range of good lessons designed to the core curriculum. You may also be able to find a variety of good free lessons on the above sites and social media, although they probably won't be quite as polished as some of the paid-for lessons. You may think that it is outrageous to pay for resources, especially if you are buying them off another teacher, but really, what is the issue? Take TES, you can generally buy a good unit of work for a GCSE module for ten to twelve pounds. This can be anything from fifteen to twenty-five lessons with PowerPoints and worksheets. The cost of this is at best two pints in a London pub or an average bottle of wine. If you have no problem buying a couple of drinks, then why should you have a problem buying resources that could literally save you hundreds of hours in planning? Many sites now offer a complete set of PowerPoints and worksheets for a whole GCSE for no more than £40.

"The lessons do not fit my school", "they are not as good as what I make" - I hear you say! Well, they are very unlikely to fit exactly what you need but they are going to give you a broad overview of what needs to be taught. You can probably adapt most lessons to your specific needs in under five minutes, as opposed to one hour to write the lesson from scratch. Most departments will be willing to either pay for the lessons or split the cost with you for the resources, and most sites will give you the money back if you are not happy with what you have purchased.

Time is the most precious thing that you have and buying your resources is a quick and easy way to gain lots of it. No more planning in the evenings and holidays, no more late nights reinventing the wheel. The amazing PowerPoint you have spent four hours on is not going to improve the learning of your pupils at a proportional rate to the time you have spent on it, especially if the lessons are only fifty to sixty minutes long. Consider how much time you have in your week free to create resources if you are going to maintain a healthy work-life balance, chances are it will be little over one hour. Do not waste hours and hours on making resources.

23 - Subject knowledge

BLUF: You need to be an expert in your subject. Spend time improving on a weekly basis, read often, attend CPD, and watch relevant documentaries. Subject knowledge improvement, alongside pedagogical advancement, needs to be a continuous process.

It amazes me how many teachers play lip service to their subject knowledge. The level of academic knowledge that many teachers have is embarrassing. You should be able to answer at least 80% of your pupils' questions, as well as add knowledge and insight to their learning well beyond the core diet of the classroom. Pupils will naturally be curious, and they will expect you to be able to satisfy that curiosity. Ask yourself – if you sat the GCSE or A-Level exam today, what grade would you get?

If your subject knowledge is poor, students will smell it a mile off. Naturally, you are not going to know everything in the whole world. If you are presented with a question that you cannot directly answer, simply tell your pupil that you either do not know, you need more time to ponder a proper response, or that you will look it up. Do not try to fudge an answer if you have no idea what you are talking about.

All teachers will have an undergraduate degree or higher in their relevant subject, but it is unlikely that you studied all areas of the curriculum in your degree studies, and if you are joining teaching many years post-university, much of what you learnt might be in the past. Even if you only just graduated, much of what you learnt could be a blur given the pace and lifestyle of university.

At the beginning of your career, buy a series of GCSE and A-Level revision guides to scratch up on your basic knowledge before reading deeper into the textbooks once you know the specification of the school you are working at. It is useful, regardless of the specification at your school, to have a good overview of all exam boards so that you can appreciate the differences and quickly adapt should your school change specification, or if you change jobs. This is perhaps even more important should you find yourself working at a school that does not teach A-level, but you have a view of teaching this further down the line in your career.

Once you are to grips with the basics of what you need to know in your subject, you need to extend your knowledge little and often. Subject depending, have a non-fiction book related to your subject on the go at all times. This does not mean you have to read it every single day, but three to four times per week will keep your knowledge growing and developing. Given you have decided to teach a specific subject, it is expected that you will have a large natural interest and curiosity around it. You then need to subscribe to relevant journals; I find for Geography reading the Economist weekly alongside the quarterly publication of the Geography Association magazine is sufficient, whilst dipping into daily newspapers and Twitter.

This becomes more complex if you find yourself teaching a subject that you are not a specialist in. Think very carefully about how realistic it will be to teach a subject you know little about before jumping in. Government and Politics and ICT seems to be particularly popular subjects for teachers to take on as a second string to their bow. In this position, you will be playing constant catch up to get your subject knowledge to where it is. You will need to invest a significant amount of time to building your academic knowledge in the given area, and this will probably have to come at the cost of the subject knowledge you build in your primary subject. Granted, I accept that in many second subject situations the teacher is pushed into it rather than willingly joining it, but you will be surprised how creative you can become with lessons when you do not get stuck down rabbit holes when expressing your knowledge of a given subject.

Away from reading, you need to get on at least a couple of CPD courses per year. Your school should be more than willing to pay for this, and if they are not, you should question if they are investing in the right areas with their budget. I would recommend paying for your own courses if not, or seeking free CPD to avoid becoming stagnant. Marking exam papers (although arduous) is paid CPD that will extend your subject knowledge no end. Local teach meets are often free or very low cost and you can find a wealth of useful information on platforms such as TES, Twitter, Facebook, and Schoology.

On top of subject knowledge, do not ignore your pedagogical advancement. What you learn in your PGCE will quickly become out of date (if it is not already), and you will need to balance what is effective teaching, against what your school requires and what is a fad. Again, a lot of this will come down to reading books and accessing information online. Your staffroom should provide a copy of TES and subscription is low cost if not. The Bristol Review, for example, provides a solid monthly breakdown of research and you can seriously improve your practice by joining a Union and teaching specific areas such as the Chartered College of Teaching.

If your subject knowledge is not what it should be, the only way to improve is to start getting on top of it. The longer you wait, the harder it will become, and the longer it will take you to build credibility in the classroom.

24 - Homework

BLUF- Consider the value of the homework before you set it and how it will improve learning. Plan when you will mark it and have a set discipline structure in place for those that fail to complete it.

Some see homework as the biggest lie in education. We all set it and many of us believe that it will make our students become better learners who have improved subject knowledge. What it will do is lead to tired pupils that cannot learn effectively in the classroom, and in the long-term, pupils that are stressed, anxious, and unable to perform under pressure.

Do you want to set homework? Most schools will make you, and without a huge culture shift, you are not going to be able to become the one teacher in the school that never sets homework. Parents often want their children to have homework, so they do not have to keep them entertained in the evenings. Make no mistake about it, students are all home-schooled. At best pupils will spend 25% of their year at school, the rest of the time they are under home-schooling and parents should take a huge amount of responsibility for the diet they receive at home.

If you work at a good school, there should be a homework timetable in place that all teachers follow to ensure that students do not become overburdened with their workload. If this is the case, stick to it rigidly and not put undue stress on your pupils by giving them extra work or homework a couple of days late. If your school does not have this, I recommend that you make your own homework timetable to cover your classes. Doing this, will allow you to have a clear picture of when to set homework, the hand in date, and what the marking burden for the homework will be. Whenever you set homework, the first question needs to be *"do I want to mark this?"* Too many teachers are burdened under piles of marking that is adding little to no value to the pupils, but taking valuable time away from you, the teacher! Next, ask yourself *"what is the value in the task?"* A poster is not good homework, tasks like essays that can be completed with Google in front of the pupils are going to lead to a false sense of their abilities. Do not set notes for homework. "There is too much content to cover", I hear you say. Well, that is your problem, not the pupils, and making notes from a textbook or worksheets so that you can get through the curriculum is a result of your poor planning and the students should not suffer for it. Consider how long the homework is going to take. It might take you thirty minutes, but you (hopefully...) have a degree in the subject you are teaching, and you are an adult. Teachers often underestimate the time it takes for pupils to complete homework and overburden them. Telling pupils to stop after thirty minutes will not help your best pupils. They will work into the night and eventually burn out. It might not be tomorrow or next week, but it will come whether under your watch, at university, or when they enter the workplace.

So, what is good homework? It should challenge the pupils and build interest and knowledge around your subject. At Key Stage Three, this can be questions, learning tasks, revision, extra reading, or more interesting tasks such as watching a certain documentary or listening to a podcast. Worried about evidencing this? Get them to write a one page review or give them a small test that can be peer-assessed. At Key Stage Four and Five, revision and exam practice are key, but again, be mindful of how this will be marked, do not overrun yourself with marking when the pupils can check the work themselves.

Flipped learning is difficult to effectively implement. Unless you can 100% say that all your pupils are going to complete the learning you have set, your lesson will flop. Ultimately, it is down to your individual school and class.

How much homework should you set and for how long? Unless absolutely critical, always give pupils at least one week to complete their homework. Anything less is unfair and overnight is ludicrous. If you are given a task, it should not go on your to-do list until at least the next day. At Key Stage Three, give pupils homework once per week for thirty minutes, Key Stage Four twice per week and up to forty-five minutes, and Key Stage Five, twice per week for up to one hour.

Remember it is the pupils doing the work, not you. Many teachers see their workload and work-life balance go out of control from setting too much homework, be smart about what you set, consider the workload burden and plan when/if it will be marked by you.

Inevitably, when setting homework, you will find when the hand in date arrives that not all pupils will have completed the work. I do not doubt that there will be a huge range of excuses thrown at you. The most common I have come across seems to be, "it is on my personal email and I cannot access it at school". It is your decision how to deal with missed deadlines. As long as you are clear and consistent with your pupils, there can be no argument. Generally, I will always grant an extension to a pupil of a couple of days if they see or email me in advance of the hand in date and explain to me that they have a good reason why they will miss the deadline. This shows that they are taking good ownership of their learning, and I accept that many pupils have a lot of co-curricular commitments alongside their twelve other subjects and family commitments. If a pupil arrives at my lesson with no homework, I give an extension until 0820 the next day. Why do I give an extension at this point? Well, you still want your pupil to complete the homework and if you put them straight in detention, the chances of ever getting the work are all but over.

I do not favour allowing pupils to complete homework in detentions, if you do this, the punishment becomes nothing more than a supervised study period. Most pupils will feel enough shame when confronted about not completing their work that they will produce something the next day. For those that do not comply, issue a one hour detention after school and inform their parents and pastoral leaders. The detention needs to be substantially more than the time expected on homework, and if they are not completing homework for you, then chances are this is a pattern across many subjects and the relevant pastoral chain should piece this together. In the end, it is then up to you how much time you spend chasing homework. Pupils at all levels must take responsibility for their own learning. You can have maybe 200 plus pupils; those who are completing the work deserve your time more than those who don't. Try not to focus too much of your time and energy on chasing up homework, this can detract you from those excellent students who are consistently handing in high levels of work who deserve acknowledgement and praise.

25 - Planning ahead

BLUF: There is nothing more important than planning ahead in teaching.

We have already touched on the importance of to-do lists in teaching. Planning ahead comes hand in hand with this. Whether you are running a digital or paper calendar, you *need* to be on top of the terms. Get the events for each term and year in place, parents' evenings and report deadlines are particularly important.

For report deadlines, you need to weigh up how many reports you are going to need to write and how long that will take. Add reminders to your calendar, i.e., "reports due in one week", "reports due in one day". Typically, you would want to aim to write five reports per day and work back from the deadline. This way you are giving yourself a couple of days of flexibility for proofreading and uploading them to the system we use to publish them to parents.

With parents' evenings it is good to have something measurable to discuss with the parents. Plan an assessment in advance of a parents' evening and allow enough time for it to be marked and ideally fed back to the pupils before the parents' evening.

End of unit tests can be put in the calendar well in advance. This allows the pupils to build towards the exam but also allows you to plan your time so you do not end up with a storm of marking at the same time, you can pace out your tests.

When planning the lessons for a term it is worth having everything mapped out well in advance, but just like the 80% solution, having a level of flexibility in place that allows for two or three spare lessons per unit will allow you to cover an area again if misunderstood or have some valuable revision time.

26 - AFL

BLUF: You need to know the pupils have made progress, not just guess that they have.

Assessment for Learning is an essential part of any classroom practice. There is little point moving on to the next topic or concept if the pupils do not understand where you currently believe they are at. You need proof of their understanding rather than just guessing or having a feeling.

At no point can you presume that the pupils will have the same understanding as you, the teacher. You are the subject matter expert, and you planned the lesson. Having a clear criterion for what you expect the pupils to learn in each lesson (whether communicated to the pupils or not) will allow you to assess if they have made the progress and gained the knowledge you expect. In the same way, you need to know where you want your pupils to be at the end of any topic or module you are teaching so you need to start with the end in mind.

Some of the most effective methods of assessing progress can be the simplest. With children, for small concepts, you will often be able to see within their facial expressions if they understand or not. With some classes, you can simply see that they do not know what you are talking about. Questioning is a good way to assess at points in the class. Similar methods such as thumbs-up-thumbs-down or red, amber, green cards can be a quick check for the classes progress. Other methods can be pre-assessment grids, mini quizzes or subject knowledge tests to check their understanding. Obviously, a test is more illuminating than a thumbs up or down approach, but you are not going to test or thoroughly examine every aspect of pupil learning.

Although the marking and feedback of pupil work is a good way for you to feedforward to the next lesson, the issue is that you likely will not be marking every book after every lesson in time for the next lesson. More often than not, it is better to address misunderstanding during that lesson, rather than waiting for what could be another week depending on timetable slots.

As you get to know a class you will be able to use AFL more quickly and effectively to know how they are progressing. In this sense, you can plan activities into lessons that are assessing and progressing learning, rather than being something fun to do. The worst thing you can do is plan around activities, rather than the knowledge or skills that you are teaching the pupils and carrying on with your plan regardless of the progress that your pupils have made.

Do not forget that you have a full class of pupils and you can use your pupils to test each other. Implementing peer activities into your lessons will allow your pupils to explain challenging concepts to their peers and as a result, progress their understanding of the topic at hand. Peer activities will often need to be planned into the overall lesson framework in advance to ensure that you give your pupils ample time to increase their understanding and ensure the task is valuable to their overall progress.

27 - Behaviour

BLUF: Getting behaviour right is the single most important first step you make in the classroom. If behaviour is not right, you will get nowhere.

Make no mistake about it, you will achieve little to nothing in the classroom without good behaviour management. It must start from the very first moment you meet your class.

The simplest thing that all teachers must do is have a seating plan for all classes at Key Stage Three and Key Stage Four. No matter how much they try to convince you that they will work well with their friend(s), do not give in to it. Issue a seating plan to your pupils on the first day and explain to them that it is non-negotiable, and it will only change when you decide. Generally, I recommend changing the seating plan for classes every term so that the pupils get the chance to work with other members of the class. You may preference sitting your pupils in a boy-boy girl-girl format - I find this gets the best out of the pupils. Sitting your pupils in a girl-boy format often kills the creativity of the class and this is not a position you want to find yourself in.

Do not overthink the seating plan. We have all seen teachers spend up to sixty minutes coming up with a seating plan based on EAL, SEN, etc. This is fruitless. Sit the pupils in any order, alphabetically boy-boy, girl-girl will do and then adjust as necessary once you know the class. It goes without saying that you should know which pupils in your class are EAL, SEN, and you can tailor your seating plan to fit this if required. You will also find pupils who struggle to see the board if not at the front, and pupils you want to have close to your desk to manage behaviour.

A seating plan will allow you to learn the pupil's names quickly it is very difficult to manage the behaviour of a class if you cannot say that pupils name to call them out for poor behaviour. Having the seating plan on a clipboard on your desk allows you to learn names very quickly without the pupils even realising that you are referencing a plan.

Presenting seating plans to a class can be tricky but should be used as a chance to set the tone. On the first lesson with the class invite them to stand silently at the back of the classroom and then call out each pupil individually and direct them to their seat. Make it clear that they should stand silently behind their desks and wait to be invited to sit. Once the whole class is positioned you can sit them down in silence. Subsequent seating plans can be presented in a less formal manner, i.e., with post-it notes placed on desks to highlight their new seat or their marked book in the position where they should sit.

At Key Stage Five you may want to allow your pupils to choose where they sit initially if your class size is small. This comes with the caveat of explaining that they are adults now, they have finished their GCSEs and you are expecting them to act as such. Clearly explain to them that should they fail to act in the manner you expect that we will go back to how it was when they were in the lower school.

Pupils crave structure and establishing strong classroom routines that never waiver from day one will pay dividends in the future, even if at first they take an investment of effort. No matter how much the class resists, stick to your guns, this is your classroom. Unless there are specific rules in your school about these things, get the routines nailed down regardless of what slack routines other teachers have.

All classes should line up in silence in a neat straight line before entering your class. Stand outside of your classroom and move all your pupils into line on day one. Wait and hold the silence before allowing them to enter the classroom. Once they are suitably poised, welcome them to enter the classroom in silence and stand behind their chairs. You should stand at the door as they enter to a) welcome the pupils (which will help build relationships) and b) give you the benefit of being able to control and have a presence inside and outside of the classroom. When the whole class have entered and are stood silently (without leaning on the desk behind or swinging on a chair), invite the class to sit, hold the silence. If the class fails to achieve this entrance routine at any point, throw the whole class out and do it again until they get it right, they will get bored of this quicker than you. Do not fall into the trap of believing that this will cost you lesson time, it will gain you hours in the future when the students are behaving and there is less low-level disruption.

In the first two weeks with a new class, focus far more on routines and behaviour management than teaching content. Solid routines allow you to establish clear boundaries with your class and it will save a phenomenal amount of time in the future.

To hold the line of the students being sat down in silence, ensure you have a starter activity on the board, with the title and date clearly ready to be copied down. Pupils should have their books, planners, and equipment out ready for the lesson. If you have taken the pupils' books in, you will find it best to already have their books in position on the desks ready before the lesson starts. This can be quickly completed by collecting the pupils' books in, in a systematic order that means once you have marked them, they are already in order to be put back on the desks. If you structure your PowerPoints in the same general style pupils should find it easy to pick out the title and date on the board. Do not underestimate how simple this can be for pupils to miss (see style section for more details). The starter can also be a good time to take the register for the class. The register can often disrupt the pupils' flow of thought and can be more hassle than necessary. After a few lessons when you know the class, you may find it more useful to take the register without calling pupils' names out.

If a pupil is late to class do not let it disrupt the flow of the lesson or the other pupils' learning. Set out clearly from day one that if they are late, they must knock at the door and wait to be welcomed to the classroom. At first, you may want to wait several minutes before allowing them in to ensure that there is a reasonable pause in the lesson flow and so that their entrance to the classroom will not cause undue disruption. Then quietly ask the pupil why they are late. If their reason seems legitimate, leave it at that and mark in your register that they are late and add a quick note in their planner. Embed this as part of the late routine that pupils leave their planner on your desk on entrance.

Pupils should know as part of your late routine that if they are late three times in a half-term, that you will put them in an after-school detention - this should deter repeat offenders. If the reason for lateness seems false or is a result of their poor grasp of time, speak to them at the end of the lesson. Avoid speaking about lateness with a pupil at the beginning phase of your lesson, it will only lead to disruption and sometimes a heightened level of confrontation in front of the whole class. If a pupil informs you that they are late because they were with a teacher, follow this up if possible. This again builds the idea that you have a strong sense of discipline and do not miss anything.

The same standard of ridge routines should be embedded in every aspect of your classroom. Use the first lesson to ensure all pupils know these routines and if necessary, practice them until you are happy and the pupils are clear on what is expected. Have pupils write on lined paper and put it in a ring binder folder rather than have exercise books. Keep paper in a green box at the front of the classroom and never move it. Having it positioned at the front means the pupils cannot go to the back of the classroom and capitalise on the time to mess around with their friends. The same should be true of where you position glue, scissors, and any other materials you may allow the pupils to access in your lessons.

A good school will have a strong behaviour policy that all the pupils will know. This creates a safe environment for teachers and pupils to operate in. However, it is possible, that there is no uniform behaviour policy. If you find yourself in this position, you need to implement your own that has the minimum burden possible on you. Encourage your department to adopt a universal policy with you, no matter how new you are to the department. The best way to deal with poor behaviour is immediately, if you leave it even a day the pupil will have generally forgotten what happened and you are back at square one.

For low-level disruption, issue respect tasks to pupils on the spot. These should be a generic task that you can have a bank of. Examples of behaviour you would give a respect task for includes chewing gum, being late, poor standard of dress, etc. The task you give them needs to serve nothing more than wasting their time. Trying to get pupils to reflect and change is a wasted pursuit, taking some time for the pupil is enough to get your point across. The task should take thirty minutes and can be as simple as lines. Set when you expect the respect task to be handed in, usually before form time the next day or they will have a further consequence (i.e., detention). Record the respect task in your mark book or other school system and ensure the pupil knows that if they receive three from you in a half term, then they will be issued with an after-school detention.

For more serious misdemeanours in behaviour, pupils will need to be given a detention. Again, hopefully, your school will have an established policy, but if not implement a three strikes and you are out policy. If a pupil speaks out of turn or commits any level of offence that you deem unsuitable in your classroom, put their name clearly on the board. This visual impact of being on the board is usually enough to ensure that pupils will stop whatever they are doing. Once on the board if they receive two ticks next to their name for further offences, they can expect a detention. Lunchtime detentions are often more effective than after school detentions as lunchtime is when they really want to be with their friends and having a break. If it is not possible within the structure of your school day to run a detention at lunch, run it straight after school instead. Twenty to thirty minutes for minor offences will have a big enough impact to deter pupils from doing it again. If you can get your department on board with your behaviour structure, you can split the detention duty between you so that the burden of having to be in a given place is diluted. During the detention, ensure that you sit your pupils apart, expect absolute silence, and if they fail to do this, give them another detention for the following day. During detention, get pupils to complete a sheet that I put in a folder labelled the "book of consequences". The sheet that is added to the book of consequences asks three simple questions:

a) What did I do to get a detention?

b) Why did I do this?

c) How will I ensure I do not get a detention again?

Then get the pupils to sign and date this, and if they find themselves in detention with me again, I show them their previous commitment to rectify their poor behaviour.
If a pupil fails to show up at your detention, then you will need to inform their pastoral leaders, form tutor, and Head of Year. The Head of Year should have a structure in place to support you here. If there is not anything in place, or you are not supported, I suggest you change schools because you are in a seriously bad school at this point. Ultimately, it is good practice to always let the form tutor and Head of Year know if a pupil is serving detention with you, but practically there is only so much you can achieve in a day. Calling or emailing home is also useful but very time consuming, so use your time wisely. Most parents will be on side and this can help, but for very poor behaviour, it is probably linked to their home life and the parents will either not be interested or they will put the blame on you.

Often more challenging than single moments of disruptive behaviour is the continuing, low-level disruption that is very hard to catch. The most common of this is persistent talking. When you have upwards of thirty children in a class, this can be very challenging, especially if you are not an established teacher at the school. If you have been through the sequence of putting names on the board and find yourself in a position where almost the whole class is on the board, then it is time to go nuclear. Do not offer an ultimatum to the class. For example, something along the lines of "the next person to speak is in detention" will always lead to it being the pupil who was not the main cause of disruption talking next. Not only will you then look like a fool, but the talking will persist. In this position, draw a box on the board and explain that every time they talk and waste your time, you will put a strike in the box and that is one minute of time that they owe you. If they even talk for a second, calmly turn around and strike the board, one minute.

No system is perfect, and you will at times have to adapt to fit your class and school. Explain to all of your classes that even though there is a three strikes and you are out rule, you will reserve the right to put them straight in a detention or send them out of the lesson if required. Just the pupils knowing this will mean they rarely exercise the right. Being sent out of class should be a big deal and reserved for moments where you need a high impact. It is not good sending a pupil out every lesson, you will simply reduce the impact it has. For a pupil to be sent out, they should have either surpassed your three strike rule, or they have simply become so disruptive that they are harming the learning of others. Being sent out should be an automatic detention and you should contact home as soon as possible.

Always remember that when it comes down to it, the pupils are kids. A zero-tolerance policy will not work with a class. I have tried this, and it was, in the end, fruitless. You are going to have to give the pupils chances and you are going to have to teach them again. This does not make you a weak teacher, it makes you strong, compassionate, and human, and it will build your respect in the long term.

Ultimately, effective teaching is all about the relationships you have with your pupils. Whenever you sanction a pupil, ask yourself, "what will this do to our pupil-teacher relationship?" Hopefully, you will have built enough respect that the impact will be had, and the pupil will take the message of the consequence of their poor behaviour away. Sometimes it will damage your relationship with the pupil, but that is life - move on. Finally, do not fall into the trap of believing that the poor behaviour of the class is down to your lesson planning. This is a huge lie in education and the message some poor senior managers in school will give you. Unless your lesson plan is totally rubbish, how your lesson is structured will have nothing to do with their behaviour - remember you are there to educate them, not entertain.

28 - Form tutor

BLUF: If you are a teacher, you will be a form tutor, but no one trains you for it.

Make no mistake about it, if you become a teacher, you will be a form teacher. This is possibly the most dismissed aspect of teacher training. Most tutors will spend anything from thirty minutes to one hour with their form a day. The chances are unless you teach Maths, English, or Science, you will spend more time with your form than any other class, this is why I am so baffled that is overlooked and so many teachers complain about it.

You should love having a form. It is your best opportunity to mould a group into the image you want for pupils to be successful. You have the opportunity to support a group of individuals and build fantastic relationships that can sustain over years. This will transfer into the classroom if you teach them for your subject as well. Embrace being a form teacher and enjoy it! An effective teacher should view their pastoral responsibility just as highly as their subject-based responsibility. If you do not like the pastoral side of schools, I suggest you become a lecturer at University, not a teacher.

I have seen a whole load of approaches to form time, tutor groups, family groups, whatever your school decides to call it. Most schools will take either a vertical or a horizontal approach. Vertical being pupils from two or more year groups in the same form, and horizontal being the structure of a single year group in a form. Both approaches have their strengths and weaknesses. Horizontal form groups create a very ridged and tribal structure towards the year groups in school but allows the form tutor and pastoral lead to tailor more specifically to the pupils' needs. Vertical tutoring can foster mentoring and friendship groups across the school and allow the form tutor to manage their workload more effectively throughout the year. For example, if you have a Year 9 form in a horizontal structure, all thirty pupils will want your attention at options time. Whereas, in the vertical structure, you may only have five or six pupils to contend with, but you will have to deal with several issues across the whole breadth of the school rather than more specific areas.

Your approach in form time will enviably vary depending on the age groups of the pupils you have. However, having a structure to form time will bring universal success regardless of age. Whenever I meet a new form, I always lay out my expectations very clearly at the being of the year, just as I would with a new class. I do not take a more relaxed approach "because it is only form time". You must maintain your standards and discipline in all aspects of your practice as a teacher. I present them on the first day with a timetable of what they can expect each day in form, and I stick to this throughout the year. Although the amount of time for form varies from school to school, most will have a block, usually at the beginning of the day, or less common, just before lunch, with a small amount of time reserved for the end of the day. An end of the day routine should always remain the same. I provide my pupils with an exercise book at the beginning of the year that they use each day for five minutes to reflect on their day. They can then answer the same questions every day - habits are the key to success, the questions are:

a) What three new things have you learnt today?

b) Name one kind thing you have done today.

c) Name one thing that has challenged you today.

d) Plan your evening so you can effectively complete your homework and other tasks. If there is still time, I often ask the form to share their thoughts if they would like to. It encourages mindfulness and gives a calm finish to the day.

A more varied and ridged structure is required for the long morning form time. Give your form the structure on the first day that you meet them and follow it throughout the year. Generally, your structure should look something like this:

a) Whole school assembly (I have never come across a school that does not have this at least once per week).

b) PSHEE (unless you are lucky enough to have this timetabled in a part of your school curriculum).

c) D E A R (drop everything and read).

d) Character development (You could run this throughout the year, starting with getting each pupil to do a presentation to the whole class on a topic of their choice. This will build confidence and soft skills. Give the pupils dates for the year so they have sufficient time to plan around other commitments).

e) Ongoing documentary (go with something like Blue Planet or other relevant educational documentaries that they should, but may not be able to access at home),

Most schools will also have a year group and/or house assembly at some point each week. Throwing in an extra session of D E A R if you find yourself with a spare day is always time well spent, and you may also like a review of the top news stories from the week that can lead into a group discussion.

Just like your entrance routine for lessons, you should expect your form to wait outside silently in a straight line until you welcome them in at the door. Once you have ensured that their uniform is immaculate, and they are stood behind their chairs sensibly, invite them to take a seat.

Other duties as a form tutor will include report writing and most likely some form of academic monitoring and oversight of low-level discipline. Do not pay lip service to these. The pupils deserve your investment in them, and it will pay dividends if you take the time to ask them how their day was or check in on their academic progress. Before report writing, give the pupils a template that covers in broad terms what you are expected to write in the report i.e., co-curricular commitments, achievements, and struggles - this will speed up your report writing no end and lead to a more personal approach.

Finally, do not be afraid to rely on the Head of Year for support. They are paid to deal with the larger issues and should be very supportive of you as a form tutor. They will probably have the ear of the Headmaster - if you are doing well and investing as a form tutor, it will pay off and build your reputation in the school.

29 - Starters

BLUF: Use these to settle your case down and get the tone right.

Starters have gone through many names - my first school called them hooks. The idea was that your first activity should hook them into the lesson. Not a bad name, but at the same time, you need to instil enough motivation into your class that they turn up hooked. I appreciate this cannot happen every lesson, but you also cannot expect to hook a class every lesson.

Starters can be used in various ways. At the most extreme end, if behaviour is terrible, they become a settler - something to get the class to calm down on entrance to the room. I remember training with someone who used to give all her classes a word search as they entered the room. Although this had basically no educational value, she swore that it was the only thing that would get them quiet, and ultimately two minutes lost on a word search could be twenty minutes gained in the lesson by having a settled class.

Ideally, you want the starter to begin after a silent entrance to the classroom, pupils stood behind their chair, waiting for you to tell them to sit down. This sets the tone for the lesson and allows you to begin with any starter that you deem productive. Some of your ability to do with will be linked to the patterns and routines embedded in the school. Although not impossible to instil in your own classroom, if it is not a school-wide policy, you need to be ready to have a much longer process of embedding it into your practice and then being able to start the lessons effectively.

30 - Plenaries and the end of the lesson

BLUF: Finish the lesson how you want to begin, reinforcing standards.

Plenaries are a form of AFL, but the key here is that they are also a way to save time and have a controlled end to your lesson. A short plenary should assess what the pupils have learnt throughout you lesson. However, it should also give the space for pupils to tidy up the resources used in your lesson, write down homework, and be prepared for a calm and civilised ending to the lesson. You want to make sure you finish in the same manner that you started with – a calm, productive, and sensible atmosphere. If you allow everything to dissipate, your pupils will either go to their next lesson in poor order, or they will have the wrong mentality when they next return to your class.

A tidy up song can be a good way to encourage pupils to get the room back in order. Also, having your pupils stood silently behind their desks at the end of the lesson is a great way to set the tone and make sure that any uniform issues are picked up on. You do not want to be sending pupils away from your classroom in a poor order or dress - what message does that send out?

At the end of the lesson, you should have a well establish pack away routine. Do not expect a smooth end to the lesson if insufficient time is given. Generally, a secondary school class should be able to effectively pack away in under three minutes, but this will depend on what equipment was used during the lesson and whether homework is being issued, books collected in, etc. To finish the lesson, all pupils should stand behind their desk in silence, as per the beginning of the lesson. Then, remind your pupils to sort their uniforms out - this is a continued reinforcement of your discipline standards and reflects far better on you for when the pupils go to their next lesson. Once they are in silence with immaculate uniforms, allow the neatest row or section of the classroom to leave first. At this point, the pupils will be keen to get to whatever is next (especially if it is break or lunchtime) and keeping this routine in place encourages good behaviour. The next time you see them the same routines should be in place and should never yield in the last lesson of the year or at Christmas. You may end up teaching these same pupils again further down the school and they must know that you always hold the line.

31 - Marking vs feedback

BLUF: Few teachers enjoy marking but it is part and parcel of the job, get it done!

Whether you like it or not, marking books, exams, and coursework is a reality of the job. I am yet to find a teacher who truly enjoys making, but if you stay organised, on top of your workload, and use the concept of "if you've only got a minute, it only takes a minute", you can keep up to date with your books.

Forget the red pens, green pens, purples pen, whatever crazy approach is going on, the work needs marking, and the colour of the pen is irrelevant. One of the main reasons to mark is to inform planning for the next lesson - did your pupils understand what you taught them? If no, adapt your lesson. Although it can be demoralising to discover the pupils have not understood what you were teaching them, it is essential you take heed of this and readdress what has been missed. This can be more complex when you get to end of module tests and discover your pupils have failed to grasp large concepts. This may need to be addressed through revision or homework rather than class time.

Feedback is a more encompassing process than marking. I see marking as ticks and crosses, whereas feedback is something that a pupil receives and should act on. This does not mean that we should fall into a trap of double or triple marking work, but it does mean that pupils should reflect on how you are guiding them to work and improve. It is worth remembering at this stage that feedback can be both written and verbal, and often it is the verbal interactions in lessons that will improve students most (do not use a verbal feedback stamp, this might just be the most pointless thing in teaching).

Feedback should help pupils to identify gaps in their knowledge and how to close them. The aim is to make the pupil more proficient and able in their field of learning. In this sense, it could be argued that if a pupil does not need any feedback, then the pupil has either been insufficiently challenged, or they have mastered the subject area! Feedback must be timely, that is why verbal feedback can be so useful. However, if you are providing written feedback, it needs to be quick enough that the pupil can still remember the learning episode. Therefore, it is so important to plan not only when you are going to take work in, but when you are going to mark it and return it. If the feedback is severely delayed, it could be that the pupil has continued to learn with huge misconceptions or gaps.

It is possible to create a school, or at least a classroom culture, where feedback and reflection work together to improve learning, but it will not happen overnight. You need to teach the pupils what is expected of them and the habits and routines required to execute it. It could be that the pupils enter the classroom with their books on their desks and they sit down and act on the feedback you have given them using criteria on the board (this is where things like marking codes can be useful). Similarly, with peer marking, you have to teach the pupils how to do this, and truly embedding it effectively into your classroom practice could take months - stick with it!

32 - Questioning

BLUF: Questioning is an essential part of your teacher armoury - it is quick and effective.

Questioning is a daily part of teacher life. Make sure when you are asking a question you avoid directing it at a single named pupil (the rest of the class will switch off at this point and therefore not be thinking). Provide some 'thinking time' for the pupils (i.e., more than two seconds and letting the first person with their hand up to answer), and finally ask an individual to answer. Better known as pose, pause, pounce. This keeps all pupils in the class on their toes. You can also allow time for think-pair-share before questioning the class, so all have had a chance to come up with ideas. Having a hands-down policy is also an effective way to keep all the class thinking and allowing others to avoid answering questions. We all know the pupils who dominate the class! This can also be avoided by using random name generators such as lollipop sticks.

Questioning is used to discover what the pupils know and can confirm if learning is happening or not. This will allow you to address misconceptions and confusion before moving onto the next part of the lesson. Questioning promotes academic rigour as well as participation. In this sense, it is important to follow up on answers asking for examples and justifications for the response given.

Some teachers like to pre-plan the questions they are going to ask, but in reality, this is time-consuming and is not dynamic - you are better placed asking questions amongst the vigour of the lesson. Things like Bloom's Taxonomy can be used to shape and progress questioning through the lesson, and mini whiteboards allow all pupils to answer whilst also being a quick and visual form of AFL.

33 - Rewards

BLUF: Rewards will motivate pupils at all levels of school.

Everyone likes to be told that they are doing a good job. In many respects, the best reward for a pupil is having their bookmarked and getting a grade that is correlated to the level of time and effort that they put into the task. In this respect, the introduction of effort grades, alongside attainment grades, has been useful in many schools. Although, it will remain demotivating for a pupil if they are putting in maximum effort and their grades remain low.

Most schools will have some sort of reward system in place, usually in the form of merits, house points, or an equivalent. You want to follow the school system for obvious reasons. Something like house points can be used to not only motivate pupils but as a behaviour management tool. Rewards should not be given for doing what you expect, but for when a pupil goes above and beyond – this reinforces your expectations and standards in the classroom. You need to start using the reward systems often and early or it will not become embedded as part of your classroom practice, and pupils will be surprised if you suddenly start to use it. If house points are given in planners, have the pupils put their planners out on their desk open on the house point page.

I remember with my first form, I had real issues getting them to turn up to registration on time. As a collective motivational method, I would promise them cookies on a Friday if everyone in the class turned up on time every day for the week. Although this failed the first couple of times, once they had won the cookies, they were reluctant to stop having them and timeliness improved dramatically.

Do not underestimate a sticker or a stamp. Pupils of all ages enjoy getting these on their work, even in Sixth Form. Postcards home are also effective at all age groups but are time-consuming. However, they are much nicer than an email, and the reality of calling home to tell a parent that their child has done a good job in your lesson today is so awkward and time consuming that after a couple of goes you will likely stop!

One of the quirkier systems we have in place at my prep school involve my pupils choosing an item out of the treasure chest in my office if they get fifty house points. One teacher has a huge array of bouncy balls that he gives to pupils when they reach ten house points, and the bouncy balls have a level of rarity based on the pattern that sees the pupils trading them in the playground. We also have a teacher who runs a currency system called Greenies. Greenies are mock US Dollars, and the pupils are given a core amount of money at the start of each term. They have to use the Greenies to *pay* to go to the toilet or buy a pencil should they not bring one in. But they can also earn money throughout the term as rewards, which can be used to buy prizes at the end of the month. The system is made even more interesting as the currency fluctuates (like the stock market) with the Greenies rising and falling in value throughout the term. This makes the reward systems a great learning tool, as well as a motivator.

If your school does not have any reward system in place, it is worth having something in your classroom. Even something as simple as giving pupils raffle tickets and drawing a prize (chocolate!) in the last lesson of each week can be a cheap but cost-effective motivator.

34 - Classroom design

BLUF: How you design your classroom will affect learning.

There are few things more exciting than getting your first classroom. The excitement around designing the look and flow of the classroom is a magical part of teaching. There are several things you can do with a classroom to help improve the learning of pupils.

a) **A clock** – get a clock (really your school should supply this) that is very clear and at the front of the classroom where all the pupils can see it. This will help you no end. Pupils, especially in this generation, do not generally wear watches. They will clearly be able to see how much of the lesson is remaining and this can be used to dictate time on tasks.

b) **Tables** – There is often a lot of different ways you can organise the tables and chairs in your classroom. Lots of teachers have their own views on how the classroom should look, from rows, to a horseshoe, to groups. Make sure you give thought to how you want your classroom to operate. If you want to promote lots of group work and collaboration, grouped tables work well. However, the cost of this is a higher likelihood of disruptive talk in your classroom, so behaviour management needs to be excellent. The horseshoe style of a classroom has always confused me, but it remains popular and is not seen as being as archaic as rows. Rows dramatically help with behaviour management and often work well for new teachers. You might like to try starting a class in rows and transitioning to group tables once you have your routines and expectations in place.

c) **Paper** – You can waste a lot of time across the year handing out paper to pupils. Have a clear box at the front of the classroom where pupils know there is always paper. Having it at the front stops pupils going to the back of the classroom and messing around. Pupils getting their own paper will save you a lot of time and unnecessary interruptions.

d) **Book box** – Collecting in books is another task that can waste lots of time at the end of a lesson. Have a box for each class and when they are leaving the room, they can put it in the appropriate box, ready for you to move for marking.

e) **On the wall** – making your classroom look nice can often be very appealing to you as a teacher. However, what is on the walls needs to be used to improve and enhance learning, not just look nice. If something is up on the wall purely for aesthetics, it will distract pupils unnecessarily. Think about how you are designing your room. What do you want the pupils to use? If you teach Geography, a map at the front of the classroom is going to add value to your lessons. Command words around the board are something that pupils can refer to when writing. In Reception classes, having the alphabet on the wall is useful - although, make sure the letters have pictures on them or you'll find yourself asking a pupil that cannot read to look at the letter 'A' on the wall rather than an apple.

f) **Your teaching area** – as much as you might want to spend every lesson, every day on your feet, at some point you will need to sit down for your own sanity. You will also find with many classes that once you have your routines in place, once they are working on a task, you will have time to actually do some other tasks, quick few emails, some marking. If you set your classroom up without a desk structure facing the class, you will find yourself on your feet all of the time, unable to make the best use of your time.

The final point to consider is keeping your classroom tidy. Do not waste your time and energy tidying up after the pupils. Make sure that they leave the room how they entered it and give time for the glue, paper and all the other messy bits to go away and in the bin.

35 - Support staff

BLUF: Support staff are the unsung heroes of schools, treat them well.

Schools are often thought of by outsiders as being an environment with lots of teachers in classrooms teaching lessons. The reality is that many schools have substantially more support staff than teachers. I often think of teachers being the Infantry - what everyone perceives the Army as being but accounts for less than 30% of the military. The other 70% are working around them to enable them and their results. The same is true in schools. Think about the number of office staff, kitchen staff, cleaners, accountants who are all working to enable the teacher to be in the classroom teaching lessons.

It is vitally important that you get to know all of the support staff in school and treat them as equals. Spend the first few weeks at a new school introducing yourself to non-teaching staff and making sure they know who you are because when you need something, these are often the people who can make it happen for you. Dropping some chocolates or wine off with the office team will always go down well and help you when your workload is running away from you or you need a favour.

If you are lucky enough to have a TA, get to know them. In partnership, make sure you figure out how you are going to work together and offer each other constructive feedback. Have briefs well in advance of a lesson so they know what is happening and what is expected of them in that lesson.

36 - Photocopying

BLUF: This is a place where you can waste inordinate amounts of time, get ahead of the game.

Most schools do not have the luxury of having lots of printers scattered all over the school. In my first school I had the convenience of it being on the landing right outside of my classroom. Whilst highly convenient, it also led to the annoyance of people constantly being around it and having the droning noise that printers make echoing into my classroom.

My second school could not have been more different - the printer was situated a good three to four minute walk away from my classroom. The option of popping out to print something quick was gone. I soon realised going to the printer even just once a day was wasting huge amounts of time as I waited for others to finish and watched as my work slowly copied.

That is when I made a robust plan going forward. With several lists of how many pupils were in each of my classes and all the worksheets for a term in hand, I went about photocopying entire terms photocopying at a time across ten classes. Thankfully, I had the luxury of an office that could easily store this, but even just a modest cupboard could fit all of this in. Set the printer to work just as you leave school at the later end of the day. Then, the next morning all of your printing for the term is done and you will only have to make occasional visits when you evaluate lessons and add extra bits in. The numbers of hours saved were huge, couple this with other things from the marginal gains section and you can soon start saving hours and hours across a year.

Learn how to troubleshoot the printer. Learning a few simple tips and tricks will save you huge amounts of time across the year. Printers seem to fail on teachers multiple times per week but often the fix is quick and easy. Getting someone over to fix it will cost you valuable time.

37 - Presence

BLUF: Presence is important, stand up straight!

Presence is an essential part of your teacher persona. We have already touched on dress. The first step is to stand up straight. The Army often talks about the power of standing up straight and the confidence and presence it gives you, versus slouching. Look pupils in the eye, let them know that you are listening to them and understanding them.

Setting the tone for your classroom starts the moment they walk through the door. Make sure you stand at the door and greet the pupils as they enter. This allows you to have an interaction with every member of the class before the lesson even begins, and sets the standard for what you expect, whilst showing them that you care about them. Some teachers like to have handshakes with each pupil as they enter, it depends on your hygiene management to whether you decide to do this or not. The same goes for the exit from the classroom; orderly fashion, picking up on any uniform discrepancies, and ensuring that they remember the high standards of your classroom from start to finish. Presence in the classroom is also very important, make sure you keep standing up straight and properly project yourself. Where can you stand in the classroom and still see all of the pupils? If you are crouching down to help a pupil, how do you ensure that the other pupils behind you are still working sensibly? Make sure you side angle your body rather than having your back to them.

The way you use your hands can also be very telling, an upturned palm suggests openness, whereas a downturned palm is more authoritative. Give this some consideration when you first start with a class.

38 - Challenge/Differentiation

BLUF: *If pupils are to progress, they have to be challenged.*

Classes are always going to have a range of abilities, whether that be GCSE grade one pupils at the bottom, or GCSE grade nine pupils at the top. All of them need to be challenged to improve. Learners who are challenged can think at a higher level and become more proficient in their field. I have always been a big advocate of teaching to the top and scaffolding down to support all learners, this way you can ensure everyone is challenged in every lesson.

One of the best ways to challenge pupils is with effective questioning. This can promote rich debate. Further, challenging knowledge requires more deep thought and is, therefore, more likely to be remembered. Challenge needs to be more than just extra work; it needs to work through Bloom's Taxonomy to enhance pupil thinking. In many respects, challenge is like we say in the Army, *"you have got to get comfortable being uncomfortable"*. With the right level of discomfort, you can learn more and progress your learning.

Differentiation and the level you need to provide it is going to depend on the range of abilities within your school, class, and subject. Maths, English, and Science are usually streamed (especially at secondary level), narrowing the band of differentiation that is required. In other subjects, it is unlikely that you will have the pupils in sets, so you may well be teaching pupils in a very wide band.

Just as questioning can be a successful tool for challenging pupils, it can also be an effective means of differentiation. As a teacher, you need to find the balance of what works best for you and your class, without creating inordinate amounts of work for yourself. Differentiating worksheets will be hugely time-consuming and if you are teaching ten classes per week, this is something that is simply not practical. On top of this, giving your pupils different worksheets can often be detrimental to pupils' self-esteem.

Some of the best ways to differentiate are simple and quick. For example, providing sentences starters to complex exam questions, using thought clouds to spark debate, allowing time for think-pair-share before asking complex questions, and having a wide range of questions for pupils to work through.

39 - SEN/EAL

BLUF: No matter what kind of school you work in, you will need to adapt your teaching to specific needs.

Some pupils in your class will require additional support, and it is your job to facilitate their specific needs. In some cases, the pupil may have a one-to-one with them in class, and in this case, you need to make sure the teaching assistant is briefed in advance of the lesson wherever possible. How your school supports SEN pupils will vary but all settings should have a SENCo who can offer some support to you. There is no one size fits all approach, and you must be adaptable to the student and the setting. You can help pupils to understand their strengths and weaknesses.

Pupils will find positive praise to be an enabler for their learning. Think about how you mark and whether lots of red crosses are appropriate, in say a Maths lesson, or is it just better to tick the correct answers? In English, you could give a list of commonly misspelt words. Work needs to be appropriately differentiated so a child is stretched but so they can also achieve. Some pupils will benefit from brain breaks, particularly if your school has long double periods. Think about how long you can viably concentrate for!

Managing behaviour can require very different approaches with different pupils and you must learn to adapt in the classroom. Like teaching any skills, this can take time and significant effort. In the most extreme cases, restorative justice can work better than a straight-up punishment of a detention.

For pupils who get extra time in exams, how are they going to use this extra time?

My most bizarre EAL experience was when I was allocated two pupils from Afghanistan halfway through the academic year. They had extremely limited English, knowing little beyond "hello" and I spoke zero Pashtun. The justification for this was that the Head thought I would be able to relate to them based on a deployment to Afghanistan… The Head of Department insisted that the school would be happy if they were just copying off the board. Easier said than done! Can you imagine moving to a foreign country and being expected to copy Perso-Arabic script? As the year went by, we made some progress, albeit more limited than I would have hoped.
There are a wide range of EAL learners; from bi-lingual, new to English, and developing English speakers. There are lots of ways you can support pupils, but a few key tips are:

a) Visual forms in your lesson from relevant pictures, to maps, and photographs.

b) Language organisers, such as tables and sentence starters.

c) Pair and group work.

d) Language flashcards.

e) Allowing opportunities to practice in English and their home language.

Also keep in mind with EAL pupils that SEN issues can be more difficult to pick up initially - be extra vigilant.

40 - Tribal classroom

BLUF: Create a team atmosphere in your classroom that every pupil can be proud of.

Most people like to be a part of a tribe or a team. That can be anything from supporting a football team to attending a church or a reading club. Having a sense of belonging is important. The same is true in the classroom. Although the tribal classroom is more straight forward to build in Primary school when you see the same class all day, you can do it in Secondary school with your subject and form group.

Like the tribe of old when we were hunter-gatherers, a tribal classroom requires trust, hard work, and compliance with the rules that are in place in that tribe. For example, as we covered in our rewards section, this could mean working with the system of Greenies, as currency in the classroom.

The leader of any tribal classroom is you, the teacher. Your primary role is to care for the pupils in front of you, but also keep order. Having a clear, and familiar environment builds relationships and allows learning to flourish. A sense of belonging in a classroom and a school are important, why do you think we have school uniforms and mottos?

You can build your tribal classroom in a variety of ways. It might be something as simple as having a nickname and a logo for your form. In class, it could be having table names, a unique reward system, or an aspect to the class that is just for them. When I was at school, one of my Primary teachers used to call us the 'tiger class', we all bonded around this idea, to the extent that we all came in as tigers on the last day.

Section 3 - Professionalism

"An officer should be comely, spratly, and above all else, confident in his own dress and bearing."

Lieutenant-General Worthington

41 - Dealing with parents

BLUF: Communication with a parent should usually drill the message home to the pupil. Never email anything you do not want to be used as evidence against you, pick up the phone often and when you need to get the parent into school.

One of the most difficult parts of the teaching profession can be dealing with the parents of the pupils you teach. I am a firm believer that the apple never falls far from the tree. Countless times I have found myself with a very difficult, or should I say poorly behaved pupil, only to meet their parents and realise why. Bad manners, poor language, and a negative attitude are learnt behaviour and this, more often than not, starts at home.

The complexity of dealing with parents lies primarily in the same spot as dealing with pupils - there is no one size fits all solution and lots of your reactions will rely on your emotional intelligence. As a rule of thumb, never take an unplanned meeting with a parent unless it is an emergency, which will usually be in the form of a safeguarding issue. These occasions will be exceptionally rare and may only occur a couple of times over your career. A parent who comes into the school demanding to see you at the drop of a hat is rarely, if ever, going to have anything positive to say and will probably benefit from a cooling down period at home before a meeting with you.

The majority of small issues with pupils can be solved quickly with a short email home – never send lengthy emails. If it cannot be said in five or six lines, it is time to pick up the phone or you risk your points coming over in the wrong way - tone is very difficult to read in an email. The next thing to bear in mind is do not put something in writing that can be used against you in the future. It is always safer to call the parent so that a) you can explain yourself more clearly and b) ensure that there is no physical evidence against you. Like it or not, as a teacher you need to watch yourself very carefully and ensure that nothing can backfire on you.

When a parent decides to email me, I will always email back as soon as possible to acknowledge the email and if the solution is not available at the time of writing, I will explain to them the steps I will take before getting back to them. I usually stipulate a time scale, more for my own personal planning than being for the parent's benefit. I always start the email with "thank you for your email, I fully understand your concerns around XXXX". By explaining the problem back to them it clarifies to the parent I can hear what they are saying and that I understand.

On some occasions, an email or a phone call will not cut it, and at this point, you are going to need to get the parent into school. If a pupil's behaviour or progress is so bad that you are at this point, getting the parent in (sometimes more to inconvenience them than to make any progress), will drill the message home to the pupil that there is an issue, and that they need to pull their socks ups. If a parent is coming in to meet you, I would recommend always trying to have another teacher present, whether that is your Head of Department or Pastoral lead, if not, it is you against the parent(s).

If having the parent into the school does not improve the pupil, or if the parent refuses to come in, this is the point you pass it up the chain either to the Head of Department or Pastoral lead of the senior management. At some point, you have to draw the line. If you are not supported, then you are at a bad school, and you should leave and get yourself to a good school.

42 – Parents' evenings

BLUF: Parents' evenings might be one of your only interactions with parents, make it count.

Parents' evening has mixed reviews amongst the teaching body. Often it depends on the school you are in to how the parent mood is, but regardless of that, it is always difficult to sit in front of one or two parents and give them an honest and open opinion on their child if all is not well.

It is fair to say that for pupils who are flying, parents' evenings are easy and enjoyable. It is always great to tell someone how amazing they are. For those where it is not going so well, it is important that this does not come as a complete surprise to the parents. If the child's behaviour is an issue, make sure you have contacted home in the past to explain this.

The same is true of poor academic standards or a history of not completing homework - make sure you have contacted home before, email, phone, planner note, reports etc. Few parents will take well to being blindsided so have your lead up in order.

Make sure you have a robust mark book so that when you are reporting to parents you can give them core data and facts that they can understand. The chances are that they are not going to understand the ins and outs of your subject, but they will understand that 30% in a test in an unacceptable score. Ensure sure some of the data is very recent.

It is always worth planning a class test near to a parents' evening so that you can evidence not only what the pattern overtime looks like, but what is happening right now for that child. If you manage to successfully deliver this to parents, make sure you have practical steps going forward. This could be as simple as handing homework in on time, or it could be more complex and require additional study.

Many schools now have the pupils attending parents' evening as well. A useful tactic is to start by asking the child how they think it is going. Few students are willing to lie or dramatically overegg their progress in front of their parents. In this sense, they can dig their own grave, making it easier for you to confront the issues at hand.

The most frustrating thing about parents' evening is if the parent you want to speak to does not show up. In these instances, follow up with an email if you can, but often the moment is gone.

43 - Staffroom etiquette

BLUF: There are two types of people in the staffroom - drains and radiators, which one are you?

If you are a drain, your attitude and words drain those around you. We all know the person; they sit in the corner moaning about how terrible every pupil in the school is and how much better the school was ten years ago. Speaking to these people leaves you feeling in one of two ways: either, "thank god I am not so negative; my life could be so much worse". Or, "yes teaching really is terrible and I don't know why I am in the profession, I will leave like 40% of teachers before their 5th year or I will embrace having a miserable career for the holidays".

The alternative is to be a radiator and omit positive energy. Make a commitment in your first year at any school to avoid negative comments - only focus on the positives until you are familiar in your environment and know what characters you can trust. Radiators make those around them feel happy, help ease the burden of a difficult lesson, and make schools a better place. Make sure you work at a school with more radiators than drains!

Make no mistake, people are very territorial in the staff room. Make sure you have your own mug - you will probably need at least two or three, and do not eat anyone's food. Go to the staff parties and get to know what is going on. A staffroom is a place to get business done quickly rather than sending countless emails, and a place to bond with colleagues. When you need a duty swap or a favour, having social connection will pay dividends.

44 - Dress

BLUF: Dress smart and have an effective system in place.

An inevitable part of your job is that you are on display - to the students, the parents, and the other members of staff. Dress to impress. People should look at you and think you are a respectable academic. Schools are now full of too many teachers wearing cheap all black suits walking around with their lanyards on looking like they are the manager of a newsagents.

Your school will probably have a dress policy, stick to it, and do not make yourself stand out unnecessarily. If you want to wear a suit, make sure it is a tailored one and navy or dark grey. Black suits should only be worn at funerals. There is also a habit of teachers wearing three-piece suits - these should be reserved for weddings, not the classroom. A smart sports coat and a pair of well-fitting chinos are perfectly acceptable. Wear a nice pair of oxfords or brogues and polish them regularly. Your tie should be simple and unoffensive - never wear a skinning tie unless you are planning to join a boy band. Shirts should be simple, white, with a simple checked or striped pattern. Black shirts should be reserved for your career as a waiter.

Females seem to have far more freedom with what to wear than men. Just because the dress code is not as prescriptive, does not mean you need to take it to the extreme. A ladies business suit or a tailored dress is more than sufficient to make you look professional. Do not wear heels, they are totally impractical in the classroom when you are on your feet for the majority of the day.

All teachers should wear a watch - how do you expect your students to get to the right place on time if you cannot. Carry a sensible and professional-looking bag (no person should carry a rucksack with a suit on). Keep jewellery to a minimum and if required, cover up any tattoos. Keep your hair well-groomed and gentlemen should either shave or have a beard. Stubble looks scruffy and unprofessional, what impression are you trying to give?

Above all, your dress should be comfortable and practical. Have your clothes for the week lined up in your wardrobe so you do not have to think about it in the mornings. Always have some spare sets of clothes so you can change for extra events such as parents' evenings.

45 - Your attendance to school

BLUF: You get over ten weeks of holiday per year. You need to get yourself into school during term time.

It is hard to know if sick days even exist in the Army. Unless you are in the infirmary, you are generally expected to be in work. All camps have a medical centre and if you are too ill for work, you are expected to be at the medical centre and bedded down.

In teaching, it is not like most jobs, you have a significant amount of holiday. The impact of you being away is huge for both your students and often your colleagues who find themselves covering your class or planning your work. Unless you are ill to the point that you are infectious and not functioning, you need to be getting yourself in and teaching your students. There is a big difference between being tired and being ill - you need to be aware of the difference

Really switched-on schools will have a GP that comes in every week to save you booking appointments. This will save you and the school time. If they do not, it might be worth registering at a Doctors Surgery near to your school. Flu jabs should also be provided by your school, but if they are not, make sure you get one!

46 - Holidays

BLUF: You get more holidays than almost any profession, use them wisely.

You often hear the moaning tone of non-teachers, "on holiday again?" and "are you ever at work?". The truth is that teachers' salaries reflect a pro-rata level of pay that accounts for the twelve plus weeks of holiday per year. The other side of this is that pupils, even more so than teachers, cannot sustain more weeks of education. In systems like the USA where the terms are far longer, the summer is over three months in length as an intensive recovery period.

Teaching goes through waves and troughs - the intensity of the term time, followed by the huge lull of the holidays. Most teachers build their work pattern towards the holidays, working at a high level of intensity before crashing in the holidays. As we touched on with attendance to school, you need to be getting yourself into school during term time unless you really cannot. Many teachers find themselves falling ill at the start of the holidays as they finally have a moment to stop and refuel after running on empty.

Holidays should be used wisely. They are your opportunity to rest and recover, and importantly, reflect on your practice as a teacher and the term that has passed. It is easy to fall into weeks and weeks of sitting on the sofa watching TV, but you will often feel better using the time productively. Holidays can be used to catch up on the latest research and read some of the teaching books that have been gathering dust on your desk. It also offers an opportunity to get ahead for the term. Although I would never condone working lots in the holiday, I find using the last week of the summer break to get ahead with planning, printing, and organising your classroom saves infinite amounts of time when the term starts and everybody else is scrabbling.

47 – Commuting

BLUF: Commuting is wasted time, avoid as much as possible

As much as you might romanticise about sitting on the train in the morning, reading a book with a nice cup of coffee and spending the evening commute marking your books, the reality is very different. Commuting is basically a mug's game. The train will be packed, and you will be lucky to get a seat. Although you will have the best intentions of marking, it is very difficult in a confined environment where you cannot spread your books out and use your mark book. Your students will have loose sheets to stick in that will fall out all over the place and you will generally become frustrated with the situation. That is without considering the 10kg of books you are trying to carry on your back or in a suitcase.

Driving is no better. During this time, you cannot really get anything productive done apart from a Podcast - you will find the journey you take increasingly frustrating as the days go by.

Many teachers talk about living near to their school as the end of their social life. However, the reality is that you probably will not see any students half as much as you think, and when you do, they probably will not want to speak to you anyway! Keeping a commute to a minimum, will infinitely improve your quality of life. It will make the early mornings easier, and it will make the return home quick and easy – this is especially key if you have a late parents' evening. Any commute above twenty minutes door to door should be treated with caution and you'll need to ask yourself if the school is worth it, or is it time to move to a new house?

48 - Assemblies

BLUF: Build your confidence and reputation.

Assemblies can build confidence. Start with small year group and house assemblies and build towards whole school assemblies.

Assemblies are something that many people actively avoid. Many teachers cannot see themselves up on stage in front of that many people, even if a year group assembly is less than a hundred students. If you see yourself progressing through school to become a middle or senior leader, you will inevitably have to lead an assembly at some point. At most schools, assemblies are a mainstay, happening multiple times per week. Even over the COVID-19 school shut down, most schools maintained virtual assemblies as a way to unite the community and celebrate achievement.

Like leading clubs, leading assemblies will build your rapport and relationships with the pupils. No one wants to be the teacher that nobody is aware of - you will fail to receive respect as you walk around the school and much of the enjoyment of the job is removed. Through leading assemblies, you will have a platform for huge groups of individuals to see who you are and what you are about. Of course, this is also a prime reason why many teachers shy away from them.

A good assembly should be short and sharp - an assembly that overruns is not fun for anyone. No matter how hard people try, technology always seems to be a problem with assemblies - keep it short, sharp, and on time. Many assemblies have now taken to showing videos, but on most occasions, a child could go home and watch this on YouTube. Use your voice and say what you have to say.

Make sure you plan well in advance and rehearse your assembly many times. At first, I used to write all of my assemblies out word for word and then practice it until I knew it confidently. This was not necessarily word for word, but enough so I could confidently speak and capture the essence of it on the day. Either the morning or day before, I would always go to the place where the assembly was taking place and I would practice a couple of more times there.

The fact is, you are not going to become good at anything without practice. Practice, build your confidence, and become a better teacher! Overtime, assemblies will almost become second nature. You will feel far more confident going up on stage and almost holding a dialogue with the school.

49 - Open days

BLUF: Open days are rarely how you want to spend an evening or a Saturday, but it keeps you in a job.

Working at the weekend is fairly common in the Army. I never really minded this until it was an open weekend at the camp, and you had to stand around talking to people about equipment and representing your job in layman's terms.

Open days are very similar to this. If you are unfortunate, they will be on a Saturday, and if you are lucky, they will be on an evening one day after school. You will probably have at least two open days or evenings per year, potentially more depending on your school. Open events are the perfect opportunity for you to prove your worth to the senior leadership team in the school. It is important that people get a good impression of your school to increase the number of applicants, whether you are fee-paying or not. When it comes to internal promotions in schools, it is events like open days that will stick in the senior leader's minds – they will consider; who is a team player? who is actively involved? who is not draining the staffroom?

50 - Emails

BLUF: You will receive a tonne of emails, reply to them at acceptable times of the day and do not let them bog you down.

It does not matter what job you are in now, emails are in abundance and they are not going away. In a normal school day, you can easily receive over a hundred emails if the communication system at your school is not disciplined. Messages will fly around none stop, from early in the morning, to late in the evening if your school does not have a firm policy on email correspondence. Hopefully your school will have clear guidelines on emails. If they do not, set your own email guidelines so that the parents and other teachers do not get false expectations of when you will reply and be available to them. You are not at the mercy of your school or teachers all hours of the day, you need to have a firm work-life balance. A good email policy should be to not reply to any emails before 0800 or after 1700. Nothing before or after those hours is going to be so critical that it cannot wait until your normal school hours. Certainly do not reply to emails on the weekend, unless it is a safeguarding matter and leave an out of office on for the holidays indicating that you will look at your emails occasionally and reply when possible.

At the same time, reading and replying to your emails throughout the day is important. A lot of urgent, unimportant emails will fly around which you will need to be aware of in order to effectively operate (The Eisenhower Matrix). There are lots of times to check your emails and claiming you do not have time is not an excuse. A quick check of your emails when your pupils are cracking on with a task, or during your breaks and free periods will stop your emails majorly building up.

51 - Clubs

BLUF: Relationships made in clubs will pay you back in dividends in the classroom.

Many schools will have a policy that ensures that you must run an extra-curricular or co-curricular club. What is important is how you approach this club and the level of enthusiasm and care you give the pupils. Pupils will know if you want to be there or not and this will impact their relationship with you.

At my first school, I used to run a military-style fitness circuit after school on Friday - I would be there after school every week at the time when, as a teacher, you are ready to go home. However, the kids loved it, they would turn up and do their session and more often than not come back the next week. One of the most fundamental behaviour management strategies you can have in your armoury is the relationship you have with the pupils. If they like you and can feel you are going above and beyond for them, then they are far more likely to behave in class and go above and beyond for you. This will, in turn, rub off on other pupils in a positive way, particularly if you can win over some of the tricker pupils.

What's more (again with the senior leadership of the school), if you are looking to promote and progress in your career, it will help to show the extra pieces you are adding to the school. Almost everyone joins teaching for the joy of working with children, so if you have a skill (or do not!), share it and help develop the young people in your school.

52 – Duty

BLUF: No one likes duty, everyone has to do it.

Few teachers would do duty if they did not have to. The fact is that you have lots of young children on site and they need looking out for. Duty is another arena where you can build or lose perception of your professional competence. The key to avoiding this is very simple, turn up on time and actually do the duty.

It is highly frustrating as a senior leader if you find yourself in the position of having to check if people are doing their duty, in an ideal world people would just turn up and do it. I worked in one school where members of the SLT would come around and tick off to check if you were on duty, and whilst I do not appreciate that level of micromanagement, I do appreciate that the need for it was there to get people to actually do their duty.

The second point (about doing your duty), is making sure you complete what is asked of you. Far too often teachers use duty as an extra social occasion in the playground with other teachers, but the fact is you have been given that role to keep the children safe.

As a Head Teacher, I have found being on gate duty each morning an invaluable way to get to know parents and pupils. As well as this, it has been a good outwardly visible way to build connections in the school, whilst also being able to deal with minor issues without the need for emails or formal meetings.

53 - Trips

BLUF: Leading trips are a big undertaking but can be highly rewarding.

When I was still in the classroom daily as a Geography teacher, the biggest undertaking of the year was an annual international trip for Year 8-11 pupils. Luckily, we rotated duties for this amongst the department, but eventually, the buck stopped with me and it was my turn to lead a trip. I took a successful trip to the Azores and although there was no additional pay for the countless hours of work, it was highly rewarding. Trips are another way to build up your professional profile with staff, parents, and pupils. Everyone appreciates how much of an undertaking large trips are, and people will remember that you have done this.

The same is true for running residential trips and day trips - they are a way to build not only your profile, but also build valuable skills. You will not be able to get through your career without leading a trip, so you may as well start early with some small day trips and build towards running larger, more complex trips.

The two major things that will go wrong is money and losing a pupil! Make sure you check, double-check, and triple check the finances before any trip. You do not want to undercharge the parents and find yourself going back to them asking for more money, or asking the senior leadership team to plug the gap. You never want to lose a pupil, that goes without saying, but make sure you have robust processes in place for keeping track of all the pupils. Do not underestimate how much administration can go wrong for a young person. I remember being on a trip to Iceland and having a fourteen-year-old pupil lose their passport, wallet, and shoes, all in the space of a four day trip!

54 - Networking

BLUF: Never underestimate the power of a cup of coffee with someone.

Networking is useful in all jobs, but in teaching, it can help you in your job and career development. Time spent networking in the staff room will pay dividends when you need a favour such as someone covering your duty, or if you need advice on how to deal with that tricky pupil.

Outside of your own environment, networking is an essential tool for the development of your career and knowledge. Social media offers a wealth of networking opportunities and the chance to share advice and resources. The thousands of lessons that are now available online can save you inordinate amounts of planning time, and Twitter can be a great place to ask advice on anything from interview to exam questions.

Networking with other teachers across schools can be a valuable way to moderate work and gain another perspective on how to teach in either a similar or completely different context. This is something that not enough teachers do, but the network of multi-academy trusts (MATs) have helped with this. If you are not part of a MAT, find a local area network to join, and if there is not one of them, now is as good of a time as ever for you to start one.

Getting to know other teachers can give you an insight into other schools, and recommendations, should a teaching position or promotion come up at that school. Many jobs are tied up before the interview even starts based on the recommendation of a reliable character within the school.

Senior leaders, often faced with complex situations, will find great value in being able to draw on the knowledge of the advice of a colleague in another school. I often find myself picking up the phone to speak to other Heads about a problem I am facing at the time. Having the advice of others allows you to weigh up the situation and make an informed decision.

55 - Socialising

BLUF: You are always on duty, do not ruin your professional credibility.

Much like the Army, teaching is a profession where you are almost always on duty. People see you through the lens of your profession. Schools are often very sociable environments, lots of people of similar ages and interests. I am not saying do not make friends with work colleagues, but what I am saying is be careful. There are two key reasons behind this.

First of all, nothing is off the record. If you go to the pub on a Friday after school, you are likely to let your guard down and start saying things you would not ordinarily comment on. This is coupled with potential parents or friends of parents being in the pub.

Secondly, and this is a classic in the Army, it blurs your professional competency and ability lead. If you are socialising with someone you manage and are the leader of in school, being close friends with them is going to make it substantially more difficult for you to tell them that they are underperforming, or that the lesson you observed of theirs was poor. We have all seen time and time again in schools middle leaders shying away from difficult conversations around teacher performance because that individual is their friend. This is coupled with the fact that if you let your hair down in front of middle and senior leaders, you can seriously compromise their professional perception of you which might come back to bite you when you are looking for a promotion.

When I was about to join my first Regiment, my new Officer Commanding (OC) came down to our training camp for a formal dinner. She turned up with six stitches above her eye, it transpired that she had fallen off the bar at an Army function after two many drinks. I worked with my OC for two and a half years and deployed to Afghanistan with her. She was always very professional at work, but at any functions we had, she would get extremely drunk. This seriously affected my perception of her and of others around her in day-to-day work.

56 - Safeguarding

BLUF: *Safeguarding is everyone's responsibility.*

The most common reason I hear someone give for why they were unsuccessful at the interview was a failure to satisfactorily answer safeguarding questions. I have interviewed candidates who have taught a good lesson and interviewed well but had a train wreck when it comes to the safeguarding questions. You will always be asked safeguarding questions; they are a statutory requirement.

On the most basic level, you need to make sure that you have read the school's safeguarding policy and the government guidance for safeguarding. In all likelihood, your school will get you to sign to say that you have, but have you *actually* read it? There is little benefit to paying lip service to it and failure in safeguarding is a sure way to get the sack.

Know who the designated safeguarding lead (DSL) is and know that you should always report any safeguarding concerns to them. If the issue is with the DSL, it is likely that you will report to the Head or the Chair of Governors, although you can always go straight to the authorities. Never promise to keep anything a secret if a pupil discloses anything to you – remember you are not a secret agent, it is not your responsibility to ask questions and probe. Avoid getting yourself into questionable situations, for example, always discuss with at least one other person in the room, or as a minimum with the door open. Be particularly careful on school trips if you are having to check rooms, always go with another adult. If you find yourself in a questionable position i.e., see a pupil in their pants, make sure you tell a colleague straight away. There is no shame in informing others, but it becomes slightly questionable if you keep such a thing to yourself.

Remember, the DSL will see a full picture of each child (more than anyone else in the school), so always report any concerns to them however minor they may seem. Finally, if you are the DSL, try to detach from situations so they do not keep you up at night. You will have to deal with some very difficult problems, and it is worth remembering it is not your fault and you cannot solve every situation.

57 - Dealing with stress

BLUF: Teaching is a stressful job.

Teaching is a very stressful job. In fact, suggestions are that only social workers are in a more stressful profession. The job puts tremendous amounts of pressure on teachers' time and family life. The stress can build around report time and inspections and drop dramatically in the holidays. In this respect, teaching is a roller-coaster of a job like no other. When in a senior leadership position, the extra pay is essentially for dealing with the stress of the role, rather than any extra work. No matter what your role in a school, you will only ever be as busy as you make yourself, but the stress and weight of responsibility that falls on your shoulders will grow.

Stress in teaching comes about from a variety of different reasons, i.e., the huge pressures on your time, accountability, and the hundreds or even thousands of humans you are interacting with each day. Teaching is a job where, without careful management, you can feel like you are always on. Your brain is still hardwired to react to the stress of running away from a sabre-tooth tiger that is trying to eat you, rather than an angry email from a parent. By maintaining a work-life balance and being organised, you will take a huge step forward towards managing the stress of the job.

Remember, stress is not always a bad thing. It can be the motivator to get you to do the marking you have been putting off, or to raise your game in an important lesson. In many respects, being aware of the stress is the most important first step to dealing with it. Having a good level of sleep, diet, and exercise will lay a foundation for you to deal with stress day to day.

If you can start to control and regulate your stress then you will become more resilient, which will allow you to be more effective in your job. Lots of this comes back to regulation, not checking your email at 2100 at night and then ending up going to bed worrying about what you have just read. You need to make sure you do not dwell on issues more than is necessary. Some of this can be regulated by having decompression time at the end of a school day, such as going for a run. Emotional regulation needs to become a habit and something you practice each day.

In the Army after an operational tour (before returning home), you are required to have decompression time where you can relax and reflect on your time before returning to normal life. When I returned home from Afghanistan, we had a few days in Cyprus on a camp for this decompression time. Even though we were all desperate to get home and see our families, the benefit of decompression was huge on our emotional regulation. This is obviously at the extreme end of things, but the same decompressions each day can help you.

During the school day, it is important to give yourself breaks. Although fifteen minutes for coffee might feel like fifteen minutes wasted, it may well be the fifteen minutes that rejuvenates you to a level that allows you to work more productively for the rest of the day. Avoid eating your lunch at your desk, this is unlikely to be productive.

Always remember, teaching is a highly enjoyable job, and although there are some lows, the highs enviably outweigh them.

58 - Hierarchy

BLUF: Rank matters less than talent.

It is all well and good being in a leadership position but unless you can actually lead, people will quickly see through you. A few good people led by a talented young teacher is far better than an old Head of Department who cannot get anyone to follow them. Schools and the Army both have very defined hierarchies.

The Army has two clear structures, that of soldiers and that of Officers. The relationship between Officers and soldiers is perhaps best summarised through the view of a football manager. The manager has the overall control and charge of the team but (in all likelihood) could not play on that team, yet they know how to best utilise the player's skills to win. The soldiers are the players, hardworking specialists fulfilling a specific role as part of the team. Soldiers can rise through the ranks of private to Lance Corporal and beyond up to Warrant Officer Class 1. Officers can go from being Second Lieutenant and Captains to being a Colonel or at the very top a General.

Teaching is very similar in some respects as you have the Officers (the teachers) and the General (the Head). In the support staff, you have the soldiers who work to support the mission and operation of learning in roles such as Teaching Assistants and Receptionists.

It is important to understand the hierarchy in any organisation, but in schools, it will allow you to understand who is making decisions and with who, as well as, who to ask permission from and how to gain influence in the school.

Where do governors fall? They are like the government to the Army. Everyone is accountable to someone and it is about ensuring you are doing the best job possible at whatever level you are at.

59 - Emotional intelligence

BLUF: You need to be the rock in the pupils' chaotic and varied lives.

A degree of emotional intelligence is needed in life, not only within the teaching profession. You are going to be dealing with pupils from a range of different backgrounds. There will be differing pressures at home and in school, with everything from friendships, academic pressure, to not getting selected for the school football team.

In an often irrational world, it is your responsibility to remain rational and look after the children in your care. They need you to be a consistent rock for them, especially when they are in a hormonal whirlpool.

Emotional intelligence is seen as focusing on five main areas:

a) Self-awareness

b) Emotional control

c) Self-motivation

d) Empathy

e) Relationship skills

Emotional intelligence is something you can learn and indeed teach to your pupils. Being self-aware allows teachers and pupils to identify their weaknesses and work on them, whilst also having the emotional control to manage feelings such as anger and despair. Self-motivation is arguably a more important trait than IQ and can be a great teller of success. It is important to have empathy for others and work to understand their position and thinking. It is vital that the relationship between teacher and pupil is carefully managed. Students struggle to learn from teachers they do not like. At the same time, if pupils in a class get along with each other, it is a richer learning environment.

60 - Know your school and its surroundings

BLUF: You need to deeply understand the environment you are operating in.

There is a huge diversity of schools in the UK, from expensive independent schools to highly selective Grammar schools and underfunded state schools. It is vital that you intimately know your school and its surroundings. Go out for a walk and a meal in the local area and observe what is going on and what the population dynamics are.

Reading online about the area and understanding the context of where you are working will tell you a lot about the backgrounds of the pupils. At my first school in London, where family income on average was below £20,000, I made the vital mistake on my first day of asking pupils what they had done that summer, the answer was very little. When I joined my first independent school, I asked the same question and had everything from a villa in Dubai to scuba diving in Thailand.

Although I am not suggesting that you teach low-income pupils differently to high-income pupils, it will help with you emotional intelligence if you have a level of understanding about what is going on at home.

It is also worth understanding what the other surrounding schools in the area are like. My school in South Croydon was nearby to a very prestigious independent school and this split the community even further. Similarly, at all levels of teaching, it is also worth understanding what the local Primary schools are like. Try and visit some if you can for the day, but if not, even driving past, going to an open day, or researching online is worthwhile.

Section 4 - Your Career

"

Train hard fight easy

"

61 - Picking the right school

BLUF: The job is very different depending on the school.

Picking the right school is absolutely essential. As we pick up on in the interview section, the interview is a two-way process, they are looking for the right candidate, but you are also looking for the right fit. Do not be afraid to say no, and do not jump on the first school you see unless you feel it is the right one for you. Teaching is one of the few professions where there are thousands of jobs across the country advertised each year.

Before going to an interview, you want to research the school in detail online. Schools usually have a shiny, positive website. So in reality, apart from a general overview of the school's ethos and policies, you are unlikely to learn a great deal. Look at other websites for further details, the latest inspection report always makes for good reading and any media coverage or comments on other websites can be useful.

Some schools will welcome the opportunity to show you around the school before the interview day. This is a win for both parties because it can remove the effort of an interview day if the fit is not right from the start. The key things to look out for include:

a) How do the pupils move around the school?

b) What does it look like inside lessons?

c) Do the staff seem happy?

d) Is the school well taken care of?

Quizzing the person showing you around is always useful and if it is a pupil, rather than a staff member, it can be even more pertinent. A lot of this will come down to what you want. It might be that you are looking for a challenging inner-city school, you might want a small village primary, or an independent boarding school. There are so many possibilities across the UK education system, you should spend your time choosing carefully because it will have a huge impact on your life.

At the same time, especially at the beginning of your career, there can just be the pressure to get *a* job. In this case getting a job at *a* school, rather than *the* school might be what you need to allow you to build some experience and shape your career towards the right school.

62 - State vs Independent vs Grammar

BLUF: There is a vast difference between state, independent, and Grammar schools, whilst at the same time having core similarities.

Choosing what sector to work in is like choosing a Regiment in the Army. The core business is the core business, teaching the children, and leading the soldiers. However, the environment, expectations, and pressures in each can be vastly different. In the Army, you can serve in a variety of Regiments across your career, if you choose, and the same is true for teaching. Working in a range of sectors will bring you a valuable range of experience.

Let's start with the similarities. Most schools across the country are structured in largely the same fashion, classrooms, departments, year groups, senior leadership teams, etc. Although deviations exist, all three sections have a largely similar approach. In the classroom, you will follow a timetable, teach a specific number of lessons, mark books and deliver feedback to parents through written reports and parents evening. There will be some expectation to add value to the school outside of the classroom whether running the netball team or taking a lunchtime club. You will have the opportunity to promote and progress your career and complete CPD in a range of different ways. That is the heart of a school.

State

State schools are the core of education in the UK. 93% of pupils are educated at a state school. I would suggest to all teachers, no matter what sector they find themselves in for most of their career, working in a state school is an excellent experience and, in some schools, it is what it is like to be on the coal face.

Classes in a state school are always larger, often up to thirty-four students, but in extreme cases even bigger. This puts routines and behaviour management at the centre of your practice. If you cannot control the class, you fundamentally will not be able to teach them in such large numbers. The range of abilities is likely to be very large, unless in a subject that streams pupils.

The higher number of students in your class will create a larger burden around marking which is particularly difficult around mock exam season. You may also find the parents you really want to see are missing at parents' evening.

Commitments at weekends and in the holidays are likely to be far less than in an independent school, but terms are also longer.

Independent

In an independent school, you cannot lose sight of the fact that the parents are paying school fees. Although the media reports huge school fees and a picture of all independent education being like Eton, this is far from reality. In fact, Eton, is far from the reality of what most of the media portrays. Independent education is a choice for parents and as such, they can always take their business elsewhere (state education is a guarantee for all children in the UK). Although schools vary in price, day prep schools are around £5000 per term and senior schools are usually a couple of thousand pounds more on top of this. Obviously, prices vary dramatically depending on the location with fees in London being higher than the rest of the country, and boarding fees adding at least £10,000 on top of the base level for fees. There are lower-cost alternatives available with some independent schools opening offering education for £100 per week. Of course, many costs need to be added on top of this, including (generally) expensive uniforms, trips, and co-curricular activities. The vast majority of parents in independent education are not super-rich but are compromising in other areas of their life to pay for independent education, whether this is a small house, an older car, or less money into their pension. This is without considering that the parents are already paying for state education for their children through their taxes.

Most independent schools will have vastly smaller classes than state schools. Few have class sizes above twenty-four. In my prep school, we have an average class size of sixteen. In GCSE and A-Level subjects, you can expect even smaller classes. Teaching Geography, I had an average of twelve pupils for GCSE and eight at A-Level. This is, of course, subject dependent, I remember a Latin class with one pupil!

Independent schools usually have vastly more resources, so paying for CPD, including Master's degrees, become less of an issue, as does buying resources to aid your teaching. However, back to the idea of parents being customers, expectations are sky high, and parents are paying because they expect excellent results and as much guidance and interaction with you as they see fit. Vast amounts of homework are expected, rightly or wrongly so, and there will be huge demands on your time.

Independent schools run a broad range of co-curricular programmes that may require you to work several evenings per week and weekends. It is not unusual to find yourself as a Maths teacher running a sports team every Saturday for the year. There is also an expectation for long and adventurous trips, whether it is a week skiing in France or ten days trekking in Costa Rica. You will have more holidays than in the state sector (usually by three to four weeks), but with the extra work required on the weekends, evenings, and holidays, this advantage quickly disappears. This is without considering that most independent schools run a minimum of an extra hour on the school day compared to a state school, meaning you are doing an extra day of teaching per week before you even start on everything else.

Boarding is another matter, although when joining a boarding school, you should have some level of expectation of what will be expected in terms of weekend and evening work. Most will be running Saturday school on top of a much longer school day.
Staff at Independent schools will get some level of discount on fees for their own children and in some cases, housing is provided at vastly reduced rental rates.

Grammar

Grammar schools mirror many of the characteristics of state schools but the key difference is that you must pass an entrance exam to gain a place. Currently, there are 163 selective Grammar schools in the UK. Tests take place around September of Year 6 for the pupils wanting entry into the Year 7 cohort. The variations for entry are extensive, including tests score and catchment area.

As a result of the test, the pupils' ability levels are generally far narrower than you will find at a state school as there is a floor level for entry. The cohorts can have widely different levels of socio-economic backgrounds and as a result, in some respects, are a hybrid between state and independent schools. They will often offer expensive and adventurous trips, but in fewer numbers than independent schools. The same can be said for clubs and activities - they will offer a variety, just not to the same degree as independent schools, and facilities are likely to be very different.

We have an amazing array of schools in the UK. If you can, try to build your career experience in all three sectors as it will provide useful for polishing your teaching practice and informing your decision on what school is right for you. They all offer their own quirks and rewards, and as always, the school you work in will fundamentally define your enjoyment of the job, or not. When I first left the Army and taught at my first school, I was questioning if it was the right career move. My second school was excellent, and I have never looked back. If you find yourself in the wrong school, try another before leaving the profession altogether.

63 - Primary vs Secondary

BLUF: Although the two are different, you can move between them.

Although you will complete your PGCE/ITT in one of the two sectors, you are by no means wedded to that sector for the rest of your life. It is not uncommon to go from Secondary to Primary, although going the other way can be more difficult depending on your degree.

The greatest take away I have, having moved from Secondary to Primary school is that the pupils are happy to see you! This is not to say that they are not at secondary school, but there is genuine happiness on the faces of Primary children that you simply do not get with teenagers. Of course, at Primary school level, you are dealing with younger children and the nature of teaching a class rather than a subject means that you will have to have a broad range of knowledge, being able to teach everything from Maths to Art. This becomes even more complex in the younger years where children struggle with zips, laces, and buttons to name but a few!

Of course, many aspects are common to both sectors. Report writing, parents' evenings, marking and exams. Most of the job is comprised of different depth levels of academia and different age groups of pastoral care issues.

In secondary school, you are going to be a specialist in at least one subject area, but commonly teachers will dip their hand into several other subjects. I remember teaching A-Level Politics with zero politics background, and it actually went pretty well considering. When you are focusing clearly on the content, it avoids the danger of going down rabbit holes because you do not have the knowledge to do it. The emotional spectrum of secondary school pupils is great, from pre-pubescent Year 7s through to almost University pupil eighteen-year-olds. This can lead to a whole spectrum of pastoral issues. The other side of this is the level of marking required, particularly with exam classes, and the depth required to develop the pupils. This is where effective and consistent development of your subject knowledge is key to ensure that you can successfully promote your pupils' progress.

Regardless of the sector, your understanding of both is highly important and spending time in the two, whether shadowing a professional, observing a teacher, or leading your own lesson can make you into a very well-rounded professional.

64 - Interviews

BLUF: At an interview, you are interviewing them as much as they are you. Do YOU want to work at this school?

At interview, you should feel like you are choosing the school as much as they are choosing you. Do not be afraid to turn a school down after having a tour and meeting some of the staff or pupils. If it is not right for you, then it probably won't ever be right for you. Now is the time to get it right, and even after the interview, you might want to change your mind. There is nothing wrong with turning down the wrong school.

Most teaching vacancies available are posted through TES. Once a position closes, you can expect to hear if you have an interview within a week, with the interview being soon after. It is far better to do a small number of tailored, well-written applications than a bulk of generic applications. When senior staff are filtering candidates for jobs at a school, they are always looking primarily for the right level of qualifications and experiences. This is then followed by a personal statement that shows some level of research and understanding of the school – this is where you can showcase your skills and experience on a more personal level.

On the day of the interview, make sure that you are on time - preferably five minutes early, but not more because that just becomes frustrating for a school when it is in the midst of prepping for the day. I have often turned up to interviews a good hour in advance to avoid any danger of being late and spent the next fifty minutes or so at a local coffee shop or walking around nearby neighbourhoods gathering my thoughts. If you are late, do not expect to get the job.

You will typically find yourself on a tour with some of the other candidates and either a member of staff or some pupils. Make no mistake about it, you are being assessed from the second you walk through the door by everyone, from the person on Reception to the Heads PA. Be polite and ask questions! Dressing appropriately is key, over smart is better than under smart - my military mind always looks for well-polished shoes. I find buying at least one new item for an interview gives me a boost, whether it's a new pair of shoes or a new tie. Do not leave your coat on during the interview, it makes you look messy!

If you are unfortunate, you will find yourself having lunch with a member of the department you are joining or senior staff. These are always very awkward moments if happening with other candidates. You will probably then have a series of interviews, usually with the Head, some other senior leaders and the person who is the head of the department or Key Stage you are joining. Although the range of questions is vast, common themes arise:

a) The school are legally obliged to ask safeguarding questions. This should be straightforward and will be an automatic fail if you do not get them right. Usually, the answer is "refer to the Designated Safeguarding Lead". However, the 5R's of safeguarding is a quick and useful way of remembering the correct procedures. These are: Recognise, Respond, Report, Record and Refer. Generally, if you are not the Safeguarding Lead or a senior member of staff, the first three R's are the most important to you as the Safeguarding Lead will be responsible for recording and referring the issue to the relevant body. Regardless, you should always follow up to make sure this has been done and always state all five R's in the interview to show that you are aware of the full procedures required.

b) Some understanding of the school's ethos and values. Are they super academic or are they a sporty school - do your research!

c) What breadth of the subject or year groups can you teach and what else can you offer to the school? Schools often see this as a good chance to tie you into coaching teams or taking on clubs!

d) How do you organise yourself? Teaching is not a career for disorganised people and how you answer this is very telling.

e) Where do you see yourself in five years? This is useful for a Head to know if they have someone who wants to stay in the classroom or someone with senior leadership ambitions. Neither is the wrong answer, but schools will want to know what they are getting from the start.

Once you have answered the questions from the interview panel, you will be expected to ask some questions. Although slightly old school, I keep a small notebook in my blazer pocket. At the interview when they ask if I have any questions, I ask if they mind me taking my notebook out and then I announce, "well you have already covered several of my questions, but I would like to ask a few more". This indicates to the interviewers that you have given some serious thought and time to what you want to ask them. Suggesting that they have covered several of your questions is a nice compliment to their thoroughness in the interview process.

Somewhere amongst all of this, you will need to teach, unless you are going for a senior position and they will likely just presume you can teach, or the school does not see you teaching enough periods to do any damage - what they are after is a leader. You will be given the general area on what they would like you to teach about a week in advance, and it is common to only teach for twenty to thirty minutes. These lessons are like a movie trailer. The members of staff observing you teach are checking the dynamics are there and that your persona is right for their school. Do not over complicate things or you will find yourself with some element not working. Do not try to teach too much, keep it simple and straight forward, and try to avoid videos (even short ones) - they want to see you, not YouTube. Some sort of short introduction, a quick task, and a plenary should work well in twenty minutes. If you can learn some pupils' names throughout the lesson, then that will always be beneficial. Furthermore, if there are any pupils with SEN or EAL needs, make sure you have prepped something to support them (whether it is needed or not, it is better to have it there). If the school haven't given you any information on the pupils that you will be teaching, make sure that you ask so you can prepare the relevant differentiated resources. This is often a test in itself and will inevitably paint a positive picture of you before they even meet you!

Most teaching jobs will give you a same day decision. Senior roles will have a few rounds and take longer. If you are offered the job, the ball is now in your court and this is your only real chance to pin down your salary at the level you want. They will know what you earned in your last position as they will have asked on your application and will check as part of the referencing process, but do not undersell your value. By being offered the job, they are showing their intent - they want you! There are a lot of schools out there - you have options. Recruitment can be a nightmare for schools so a couple of extra thousand pounds on your salary could be very achievable.

Finally, if you do not get the job, do not be disheartened. It might not have been the right school for you, and you might not be what they are looking for. There might have been another candidate who was more affordable, or sometimes a candidate was lined up in advance and the whole thing was a dance.

65 - Salary

BLUF: The teachers who make the most money are the ones who move schools, take on the responsibility or ask for it.

Let's be honest, no one gets into teaching for the money. Most individuals could earn more money in other professions, just with substantially less job satisfaction, meaning to their life, and fewer holidays! However, there is good money to be made in the profession. Although an ECT starting salary is relatively low, you can quickly double, and even triple your salary (certainly inside a decade) by taking on more responsibility and asking for more money. Some of the top Executive Heads earn over £200,000 per year, and it is certainly not uncommon for Heads to have six-figure salaries.

When you start, you are going to be on an ECT salary with little room for manoeuvre. However, you can always try to negotiate, especially if you have additional qualifications like a Master's degree, or if you know that they are struggling to recruit. From here, a pay rise in school will most likely be incremental to a point, but you can always earn more money through taking on extra responsibilities.

In many cases, you will find yourself taking on more work to prove yourself at first, but this will pay dividends when you do ask for a pay rise or pay rises are given. I found myself running bronze DofE at my first school and it paid dividends when negotiating pay at my next school.

Moving schools is one of the best ways to increase salary. You are often in a far better negotiating position than at the school you are currently at. Many of the higher salaried teachers have managed this by moving schools every few years and negotiating their salary up. This is a workable solution because you find yourself with a job, but also the offer for a job that wants you and is going to have to pay at the very least what you already earn.

Having said that, do not be afraid to go and ask for a pay rise if you can justify why you deserve it. If you are going above and beyond, you are likely to be positively received as long as you are not asking more than every couple of years.

As you take on more responsibility, make sure that you are getting the salary increments for it. Some schools will try and get you to take on more work without any remuneration. This is not fair. Before you know it, you are doing more work than others for a lot less pay. Although, teachers are often very closed about how much they earn.

As you progress to middle leadership, you should see your salary reach over £40,000 and with Senior Leadership often around £70,000, depending on the location and size of the school.

The final thing to think about is the benefits that come with the job. Make sure that there is a good pension in place. Many schools will offer free gym membership, private health care, and IT equipment. Schools will also pay for CPD and often part or all of Master's degrees. In the independent sector, it is not uncommon for schools to offer at least a 50% discount on school fees, which with multiple children, can be a huge bonus on top of your salary.

66 – ECT years (formerly known as the NQT year)

BLUF- Plan weekly meetings with your mentor and stick to them. Book thirty minutes per week into your teaching timetable to complete weekly ECT administration tasks.

It is important to recognise the introduction of the term 'ECT' (Early Career Teacher) replacing the formerly known NQT year. This new term for NQT is being implemented from September 2021 which provides a two-year programme of high-quality professional development for new teachers.

This reform is driven by the aim to improve the training and development opportunities available to teachers. For example, a 10% reduced timetable in your first year of teaching, and a 5% reduced timetable in your second year.

There are some fundamental elements that will lead to success in your ECT years, and by success, I do not mean simply passing your two years. Success is setting the conditions for your future happiness as a teacher. You should not be a stressed, overworked teacher with no social life, and this needs to start in your ECT years.

Do not start by committing to having one night off from work per week, as many promote. Commit to having every night off. When you leave work, you leave work. There might be exceptions to this, but I find this is no more than two to three times per year at the real pressure points, i.e., end of year exams and reports. Do not make a habit of working late into the evenings, if you do, you will rely on that time to complete your workload - you can get everything done at school without staying late.

Having a good mentor will make your two years far easier. However, you will be assigned your mentor and the quality varies from amazing to terrible. You may find that your mentor is uninterested and has taken on the role as your mentor through force rather than choice. Make sure you organise a time to meet your mentor on a weekly basis and stick to that time all year. Having thirty minutes to one hour with a person each week to unload and discuss your teaching practice is invaluable. Nothing should take president over this time and do not let the meetings slip, your teaching will suffer if you do. Your mentor will have a reduced timetable to allow them to meet you, and if you are at a good school, this will already be planned in.

Regardless of your mentor, you need to take a "no cuff too tough approach". In that sense, I mean act fully confident, stay calm and in relative control. This does not mean do not ask for help. It means do not run around your department giving the perception that you are unorganised and unnecessarily stressed. Although your observations and your evidence folder are your formal methods of assessment against your ECT years, it is everything else around it that build the perception, to your mentor and others, that will determine how you are perceived in your school. In the future, if you want to progress up the ladder in your school to be a Head of Department, Head of Year or beyond, your perception from the start of your time at the school matters. Obviously, if it all goes badly, you can always change schools and start again, but that means new routines, new systems and new people, all of which will make your life more difficult.

Throughout your teaching career, organisation will be one of the most fundamentally important parts of your teaching. Keep on top of all your ECT administration, do not leave it all until the end of term to start evidencing your folder and tracking how you are meeting the standards. If you do, it will take you a phenomenal amount of time and you will struggle to effectively evidence and remember everything. Set aside twenty to thirty minutes a week to complete ECT administration, this is partly why you have a reduced timetable for two years. Add that slot to your timetable and protect it. No matter what, always ensure that you organise your workload so that you never have to run into this time - avoid the temptation or suffer the consequences later.

67 - Making your life easier

BLUF: *With a little investment, you can make your life a lot easier.*

In the Army I used to budget £100 (minimum) in kit for any field exercise. Although the Army supplies you with all the basics you need, somethings just make life that little bit more comfortable and therefore that little bit easier and more enjoyable. Typically, this would include a decent flask, good pairs of walking socks, and a smaller but more insulated sleeping bag.

Schools will provide you with the basics and many will go far above and beyond this. For example, some schools will provide you with an iPad or a laptop, free lunches, and what feels like an unlimited supply of stationery. I appreciate that most teachers are on modest salaries, but marginal gains. made with a little bit of investment can make your life infinitely easier. Having your own laptop will allow you to multitask in class whilst also giving you the flexibility to work in any part of the school (particularly useful if you do not have your own classroom or office), and you could run online mark books and lesson planners. Although investing £500 plus in a decent laptop might seem extravagant, it will save you a huge amount of time that will allow you to keep that all-important work-life balance in place. A USB stick with all your lessons on can also be useful if you are changing classrooms and having to jump between machines. Using cloud-based storage always sounds great until the internet is so slow in the classroom causing you to waste vital lesson minutes waiting for the site to load.

For the less digital amongst you, a decent teacher planner is well worth the investment, specifically ones that you can personalise to include the right number of periods and bespoke to-do lists.

I invested about £150 into my first classroom to make it look like an inviting and interesting learning environment. As much as anything, I knew I was going to be spending about five hours a day in the room and I wanted it to be a nice place to work. It was well worth the small investment.

The same goes for lessons resources you might want, but the school cannot pay for. For many subjects, a subscription to 'The Economist' or 'The Week' proves to be a valuable lesson resource. Membership to subject associations offer their weight in gold in CPD – a little bit of investment can go a long way to making your life easier.

68 - Annual Review

BLUF: This is your one chance to showcase and record your successes, do not let it go to waste.

I am amazed at how many staff pay lip service to the annual review process. Although schools run a range of annual reviews, from 360 degree, to horizontal and vertical reviews, all schools should have some system in place.

This is your chance to record and highlight all your achievements in the year. Much of what you do may go unseen, i.e., is your line manager aware of all of the hours that you give to a particular sports club or the time you have spent away on the Duke of Edinburgh's Award? These types of commitments to the school are often unpaid but will help with promotions internally. Alternatively, they will allow you to build a notable teaching profile to apply for promotions at other schools. More than that, they are an enjoyable part of the job that allows you to build relationships with the pupils.

When the input for your annual review arrives, knowing teaching, you will be busy and tempted to pay lip service to this, brushing over many of your achievements. Over your PGCE and ECT years, you have to keep heaps of evidence to highlight your progress, most of us stop this after the initial induction period. However, some of the habits learnt in the early years are worth hanging onto for annual appraisal. Keep a list of everything above and beyond that you are doing in your job role and the date that you do it. This could be anything from running Earth Day, to helping children with a bake sale. Although they may seem insignificant, they all add up and build a great picture of your body of work. At the same time, sitting down and trying to remember them all at once can be difficult.

Finally, it is always worth highlighting your short, medium, and long term ambitions. Many promotions are tied up before the interview as the school already has someone in mind. If you aim to be a Head in the future, maybe the sitting Head can help you get there, do not miss your chance!

69 - Teaching Unions

BLUF: Join a union - it does not matter which, just join one. You will probably never need it, but if you find that you do, then you will really need it.

Joining a union is like house insurance, you are unlikely to need it but when you do, you do! Most Unions run membership for free or a substantial discount for PGCE students and ECTs - sometimes these discounts run into your first couple of years of teaching. After that, you are generally looking at around £20 per month for membership.

The first thing to note is that membership brings lots of CPD and networking benefits. Lots of course and conferences run throughout the year and as a member, you get priority entry to these alongside access to extra pieces on websites and usually a magazine.

On a more sombre note, they are essential if you find yourself in a difficult situation. This could be anything ranging from wrongful dismissal from your school or an accusation from a student. Union support here is vital, giving you support, often from a legal perspective that could run into thousands of pounds. Make sure that you get membership in place early and always remember that you can switch Unions if you feel like they no longer represent your interests.

70 - Doing CPD

BLUF: CPD is your responsibility, no one will hand it to you.

CPD is a great way to improve your career and improve your overall knowledge. Lots of teachers miss out on CPD because no one is making you do it, and there is no requirement to complete most courses for promotion. In the Army, you have lots of core courses to complete to progress through your career, and although they have tried this in teaching, particularly with the NPQH (National Professional Qualification of Headship) it has never caught on under the constraints of budgets and cover within schools. Other NPQ courses include in middle, senior, and executive leadership. The independent school equivalent is the Independent Schools Qualification in Academic Management (ISQAM).

Most schools will have some level of CPD budget, and you should make sure that you get on board with using some of it. Having said that, there is a lot of good CPD out there, particularly through Universities. Ensure that you stay connected to the Universities you studied at to access these.

Be proactive in finding courses and get your requests in early to make sure that you can get on them before department or school money runs dry. As you move through your career, the type of CPD you need will change, i.e., the skills you need in ITT are distinct from the middle of your career.

Broadly speaking, the three key CPD areas are:

a) In the field– going into another school

b) Academic – university or institute led courses

c) Professional – mentoring, coaching, reflection

CPD is also good for your overall wellbeing. Having a couple of days a year out of the classroom to learn and network will do you the world of good and refresh and prepare you for the rest of the term or year ahead.

71 - Leading CPD

BLUF: leading CPD puts you at the forefront and develops your standing in the school.

Like building your confidence through taking assemblies, leading CPD is a good step in your career. It puts you front and centre amongst your peers and takes you out of your comfort zone. In some respects, CPD is the most beneficial for the leader of it, as they have done all the planning and additional research. Most schools have at least five INSET days per year and few can afford to fill them all with externally led training. On top of this, schools will run evening twilight sessions or even weekly CPD.

Leading CPD, whether it is coaching and mentoring or more traditional up on stage with a PowerPoint, CPD allows you to showcase your skills and knowledge to the whole staff body. It allows the CPD to be directly relatable to the school and vitally for senior leaders in charge of the purse-strings, it is free.

Should the opportunity arise to volunteer to take a CPD session, you should jump at it, and as a senior leader it should become part and parcel of your business. When leading CPD, you should be considering what you are going to achieve - start with the end in mind! You will want to see all or some of the following:

a) Staff feel they can use the knowledge you have given them to change student outcomes

b) Staff have personal growth

c) Time for reflection

d) The CPD is part of a sequence rather than a one-off, stand-alone, session

Perhaps point three is the most important. Time to reflect is rarely made available in teaching and CPD offers a prime opportunity for this.

72 - Doing a Master's

BLUF: Doing a Master's degree will help you progress through your career quicker.

Increasingly, schools are looking for people with Master's degrees, particularly for SLT positions. If you want to be a Head, a Master's level degree is almost essential now so that you can show you have the higher-level knowledge to take a school forward. MA

(Master of Arts) remains the most popular Master's degree, giving teachers a distinct set of teaching skills that they can use to develop teaching and learning in a school.

In recent years, Master of Business Administration (MBA) degrees have started to become popular amongst Heads, as Executive Heads and Independent school Heads, in particular, find themselves in charge of multi-million-pound budgets.

The key with a Master's degree is not to do one for the sake of it, but to do one with an end goal in mind, whether that is a promotion or the advancement of your skills. You are X more likely to progress to Head of Department with a Master's degree than without and this has consequences for the speed that your career progresses and in most instances the pay you receive.

Many schools will sponsor you through a Master's degree, paying some, or all of your fees. It is always worth asking. It is manageable to complete a Master's alongside working, just remember the 80% solution and "if you've only got a minute it will only take a minute".

73 - Doing a Doctorate

BLUF: A doctorate is a next step up with only 0.4% of teachers having one.

A doctorate is a big undertaking and limited numbers of teachers have a Doctorate. Even amongst the 0.4% are career changes into teaching rather than completing a Doctorate on the job. Having said that, if you are brave enough to take on a Doctorate over four to seven years, a couple of routes exist. A Master's degree is almost always needed as a pre-requisite, at a minimum merit level.

A PhD is research and theory driven and is more geared towards a career in academics. An EdD is the other type of Doctorate that educators undertake and is more commonly associated with those who are practitioners within schools. Either is a huge commitment but can significantly develop your knowledge and skills.

Doctorates are also a good way to give yourself future career options. An increasing number of teachers are finding it difficult to find the energy to work well into their sixties to pensionable age, so the option of working in consultancy or academia with a Doctorate can be appealing.

74 - Middle leadership

BLUF: Setting into middle leadership will allow you more control and influence in the school whilst developing your leadership skills.

Almost 40% of teachers in the UK are in middle leadership positions. The vast majority of teachers, at some point or another, enter middle leadership whether as a Head of Year, subject, Key Stage or one of the other weird and wonderful positions that schools have created. Some schools have a middle-ground approach with assistant heads of departments and year groups. This is a low-risk way to shadow the person in charge whilst developing your practice. Remember, you can learn as much from a bad leader as a good.

How middle leadership is approached varies from school to school and person to person - some see themselves as the leader of the team whereas others see themselves as the academic expert or primus inter pares. Like Corporals in the Army, middle leaders are the engine room of any school operation. In an ideal world, senior leaders in the school will help develop the middle leaders, but more often than not, it is the individual who must take responsibility for their professional development.

Middle leadership is an area to develop your leadership skills and find your style and grounding. It is often a phase of great learning before stepping up to senior leadership or retiring back fully to the classroom. At the same time, many find that middle leadership offers the perfect balance between teaching and leading, often seeing senior leadership as too removed from the classroom.

Most teachers are promoted to middle leadership based on their ability as a teacher, rather than a leader. Although there is common ground, such as an ability to organise yourself, being a good teacher does not necessarily make you a good leader. You must seek to develop and expand your knowledge whether through reading leadership theory or undertaking courses. Goods schools will have a function in place to develop the school's leaders in-house. Few PGCEs have any leadership focus so teachers must work to put a foundation in place, whilst also remembering that there is nothing like on-the-job experience for practice.

Middle leadership is distinct from being a middle manager, as a leader is expected to inspire some level of confidence. Some schools still use the term 'middle manager', but it seems to be a dying approach with many of these roles now being replaced with a *Director* title. Being a middle leader is in many respects more challenging than being a senior leader as you must try to manage a heavy teaching load alongside your other responsibilities. Most senior leaders will have no, or very limited, classroom duties as they tackle strategic issues for the school, leaving operational matters to middle leaders.

75 - Pastoral Roles

BLUF: Pastoral roles are your chance to make connections and develop pupils.

Everyone is a pastoral leader to some extent, either as a form tutor or a class teacher. The lines between academic and pastoral roles are increasingly blurring and it is important to get experience in both rather than seeing the experience as a one or the other situation.

The typical pastoral leadership role will be as Head of Year. Most schools still run a horizontal system, defining the pupils by which cohort they are in. In some schools, the year group leader will remain with that year group as they progress through the school and in others, the person is static. Both have their upsides and downsides. Staying with pupils over five years allows you to get to intricately know them and their parents. On the flip side, you are stuck with potentially difficult pupils for five years. In the case of remaining static, you have the benefit of only having them for the single year allowing for rapid progress and pressure where required, but this can also lead to difficulties building relationships and getting to know the pupils.

Some schools now have vertical models built around a mix of year groups being in the same form and house so that relationships can be built across the school. This can lead to a more collegiate atmosphere in the school and see mentoring and development take place amongst older and younger pupils. However, this sometimes leads to no one truly having a grip on each year group and the unique challenges each face, i.e., Year 7 transition and settling in, Year 9 hormones, and Year 11 GCSEs.

Many of the systems in place will have one or more deputy heads of year or house, and larger schools often split into lower, upper, and middle schools, giving a level of continuity to the year groups under a single section head.

A natural step from a Head of Year position is often to a Deputy Pastoral role on SLT. This role often encompasses being the DSL so getting a high level of safeguarding experience is essential from a professional and career perspective.

Often, being a pastoral leader is a position of disciplining pupils and maintaining standards. However, if managed correctly, you will spend time building relationships with a wide range of pupils and celebrating the academic and co-curricular success of your pupils.

76 - Academic Roles

BLUF: The subject matter expert in a department.

Being an academic leader is distinct from being a pastoral leader as the focus is more indirect to the pupils. Lots of the role is spent leading the teachers in the department rather than the pupils. Heads of a subject department can be seen through many guises; whether in simple terms it is the person who does the administration for departments such as contacting exam boards and leading trips, or in a more professional sense as the subject expert.

There is a huge range of exam boards and specifications that you can teach and increasing levels of freedom away from the National Curriculum. It is always more beneficial if the Head of department is the subject matter expert, knowing the exam board intricately and having an enthusiasm for curriculum design.

The value of marking exams is huge. It is some of the best CPD available whilst also taking up inordinate amounts of time, often for limited amounts of financial reward. It will give you a deep understanding of the exams and be invaluable to you and your department.

Some schools have now created a faculty model that takes several departments under a single umbrella, for example, Humanities encapsulates Geography, History and RE. This can be a big step up from being a Head of Department – in some cases, a single person is leading the three subjects which presents significant challenges and makes the role more administrative than subject specialist.

A natural SLT step from here is to be a Director of Studies. A Master's degree can help in this role to build a wider understanding of teaching and learning in schools.

77 - SLT

BLUF: Prepare to manage adults and have difficult conversations but with a lot more influence.

Joining a senior leadership team or SLT is the last step before becoming the Head. Some schools still use the term 'Senior Management Team' (SMT), but SLT is the most universal. If you want to have a large level of influence in a school, you need to be on the SLT. The roles usually come with significantly more pay and time out of class (of course, this is school dependant).

Being on the SLT is a big step in any teacher's career because it takes you more out of the classroom and further into management. Usually, this is the management of adults rather than pupils and for this reason, many people are put off the idea of becoming a senior leader. In most cases, it is also much more difficult to maintain friendships with the staff body, and your job is certainly far more straight forward if there is a clear dividing line between the two. This takes on a whole new level if you become Head and you generally need to keep a line between you and the SLT and the staff body. Like the Commanding Officer at an Army Christmas party, you respectfully turn up late and leave nice and early so the staff can relax and get the party going. For this reason, it is often easier to transfer onto an SLT as an external candidate than an internal candidate as the pre-existing relationships are not there.

Make no mistake about it, managing adults has a lot of challenges and the level of incompetence displayed by many individuals will never fail to surprise you. One issue is that teachers are often used to being the king of their own castle (their classroom) and find it very difficult when anyone tries to enter. As SLT you must have the difficult conversations with people that others do not want to have. Often highly frustrating situations that would not have reached your level if there was a clear alternative. However, like many leadership situations, there is not a right or wrong answer, just the need for direction.

It is easy for lots of principles to go out of the window when you join the SLT. In particular, work-life balance - you must maintain a good level of self-care so that you can be most effective in your job role but an element of working in the holidays, especially the summer, is inevitable.

Meetings can end up overbearing your life. A useful way to avoid this is to work out what everyone is paid on average per hour and then work out the cost of calling the meeting. This will get you thinking about the time you use! Meetings should often be used to make final decisions, with relevant information circulated in advance of the meeting, not presented there - of course, there are exceptions to this.

In the end, it is a fine balance between showing your leadership and authority whilst maintaining a sense that you genuinely care for the staff and want the best for the school. Toxic leadership must be avoided at all costs, but in many respects being weak and indecisive is just as bad.

78 - Governorship

BLUF: A chance for you to develop whilst imparting some of your knowledge to help others.

Being a governor is one of the best pieces of free CPD that is available. It gives you a deep insight into a school whilst also allowing for greater influence. Some suggestions are that governors are the largest group of volunteers in the country. You can be a staff governor at your own school or a co-opted governor at another school. Other systems do exist, for example, MATs have trust boards and parent governors.

The governing boards have a range of roles and responsibilities with the Chair of Governors leading and various other roles such as the lead on the curriculum, safeguarding, and SEN to name but a few. Usually, governing boards will meet on a half termly basis with key agenda items throughout the year. Most governors will be expected to visit the school on at least a termly basis and attend key events where possible, such as prizegiving and carol concerts.

The governing body is there to provide checks and balances on the SLT and especially the Head. Everyone is accountable to someone! Although Heads are often seen as having a lot of freedom and influence in their job, the governing body keeps that in check and are ultimately responsible for the school. For these reasons, it is important to join a school to remain in post for at least four years, to offer stability and have an opportunity to get to know the school.

Although an interesting role whatever your job in society, as a teacher it is fascinating to see the inner workings of a school other than your own. Although many of the same issues exist, budgets and behaviour etc. Many challenges will be unique to that setting and the cohort of children that the school has. It is a role where you can learn a great deal to take back to your practice and school, as well as offering advice and guidance to the setting that you are a governor in. As the Head of a Primary School, I enjoy being on the governing board of a secondary school to get a different perspective, along with the fact I am a governor at a Grammar School and Head at an Independent School.

79 - PGCE/ITT Applications

BLUF: You can do a PGCE almost anywhere in the country, find one that is near to where you want to have your first job.

The PGCE application process can be a daunting task, getting it right is the first essential part of your teaching journey. The UCAS teacher training website is where you will submit and track your application and its progress - the site opens for applications each year around mid-October. You should aim to apply as early as possible before the influx of applications come in, this way you can get an advantage in the process.

There are two stages, most people succeed in stage one – this is done through UCAS where you get to apply to three different universities. You will only enter stage two if you get rejected from those three universities, then you will be allowed to apply to universities directly. Much like when applying for undergraduate studies, you must upload various personal information, references, and (most importantly) your personal statement. Your personal statement is an integral part of your application and it is the first chance you get to demonstrate your abilities to the universities so they can make the important decision in offering you an interview. Your personal statement is limited to four thousand characters which is roughly around the five-hundred-word mark.

Therefore, it is important to say exactly what you want to in the most clear and concise manner.

The most important things you should include:

a) Why do you want to be a teacher?

b) What qualities do you have that a teacher possesses?

c) What are your reasons for wanting to teach in a primary/secondary setting?

d) For secondary PGCEs, why did you choose your specific subject? What do you enjoy about it?

e) Why did you choose a school-based/university-based route?

f) What work experience have you done? Include examples.

g) What wider experience have you got that can help in contributing to your future teaching role?

Avoid clichés at all costs. Saying things like "I've wanted to be a teacher for as long as I can remember" will not allow you to make an impact and separate yourself from the rest of the applications. You want to stand out, so including general statements needs be avoided. Be unique and talk from your own passion and experience, this will allow you to write a strong and successful personal statement.

The earlier you apply, the quicker you will hear back from the universities. They have forty working days to get back to you with a decision. You could be expected to go in for an interview as early as the next week, so make sure you're prepped and ready!

80 - PGCE/ITT Interviews

BLUF: Prepare in detail and make yourself stand out.

The interview process is different at each university so there is no set standard procedure. PGCE interviews tend to last around a few hours, and they could expect you to do a range of different tasks.

Some examples include:

a) An individual interview (this is a definite) – they usually last around twenty minutes and could either be 1-1 or in front of several interviewers.

b) Group task - i.e., collectively marking a pupil's work and discussing the strengths and weaknesses of this.

c) Presentation – i.e., a two-minute presentation discussing the pastoral role of a teacher.

d) Subject knowledge test – revision is absolutely key here! You could be asked some highly specific questions in either an interview format or as a written task. I.e., for English PGCE students, "choose any poem from the Renaissance era and explain how you would teach it to a Year 10 class". Tip: Study the national curriculum for your subject – this will help you formulate and add purpose to your answers.

e) General literacy/numeracy test

f) Proof of academic qualifications

To succeed in your interview, you need to revise and prepare around the above points. PGCE interviews are far from straight forward and it is essential that you are up to date on your subject knowledge as this will be tested. Your subject knowledge could be examined through a test, your individual interview, or both. Questions could range from simple subject questions to highly specific questions on a distinct area of your subject. Revise any area of your subject that you are not up to date or familiar with. Particularly regarding what your university course consists of as it is likely you will have told them your university modules; therefore, they may purposely ask you questions relating to them.

Making sure you are knowledgeable of the current National Curriculum is also important as well as being aware of current educational issues, this will set you apart as it shows you are already involved in the teaching industry and taking wider steps to your teaching career.

Your PGCE interview should centre around professionalism in both your mindset and the way you dress. Go to your interview in a professional outfit, much like what you could see yourself wearing day-to-day as a teacher. Show your personality, you don't want to seem scripted or false. Being natural and true to yourself will set you apart and help the interviewers visualise you on the course much more accurately.

Section 5 - Leadership

"

Leadership is the capacity and will to rally men and women to a common purpose and the character which inspires confidence.

"

Field Marshall Montgomery

81 - Either lead, follow, or get out of the way

BLUF: In many ways, a good leader and a good follower are the same.

No matter what your level of authority, everyone answers to somebody. Whether you are the Prime Minister, Chief of the General Staff, or a Head Teacher. They all lead but at points they must all follow. Leadership is highly written about and all leaders should read leadership theory. One of the greatest leadership issues in teaching is that people are often promoted to lead a department, or a year group, for example, based on their teaching ability rather than their leadership qualities. Many things have looked to address this such as the National Professional Qualifications, but this has only taken leadership deficiencies so far.

The idea of lead, follow, or get out of the way is simple. If you are not leading, you are therefore following. A leader is not a leader without a follower(s) and given that most people both lead and follow, you need to be able to transition between the two roles effectively. Leaders need to make sure their followers contribute to the success of the team, no one wants a sheep who is there to mindlessly follow direction. Followers must support the leader but also uphold the integrity and the ethos of the organisation – the school and education. As a follower, it is useful to understand why a leader has made a decision and think critically about it, whilst also being clear on the direction. In many situations, there is no right or wrong direction, the situation just needs direction, and an effective follower will appreciate this rather than creating noise and distraction for little or no gain.

This is why, if you are not leading or following, you need to get out of the way because you are not helping the situation. You are hindering what is happening and in teaching, almost more than any other profession, time is very precious and needs to be effectively used.

82 - Core Leadership

BLUF: If you want to progress, you will often find yourself going down either the pastoral or academic route, the key is to seize the initiative.

The most important leadership skill is the ability to lead yourself. We all know the person that we would not follow to the local shop let alone follow in something that could shape your career or reputation. Leading yourself comes down to making sure that you have the personal skills in place outlined in section one.

Once you have these skills in place, you are ready to progress as a leader. This could mean taking on middle leadership roles such as Head of Department or Head of Year. In every position of leadership, from Head Teacher to Head of Department, you are going to have someone taking checks and balances on your performance.

At the top level, it is the school Governors but could also include a wide range of the school middle and senior leadership. That is why being a good leader also means being a good follower. The characteristics of a good follower are often the same as a good leader.

In so many situations the answer is far from clear, a good leader will give direction. At Sandhurst, this starts with Platoon attacks where you have three options - go left, right or down the middle (down the middle is never the correct option!). Deciding to go left or right is reflective of so many daily situations in schools. There is no right or wrong way to go, but as the leader, you need to give the direction and execute the plan.

As a follower, you need to support the decision and help the leader achieve their aim. This does not mean blindly follow but it does mean do not create any unnecessary level of hassle. I have sat in so many meetings where a decision has been made and despite this, others will still argue the plan rather than appreciated the key was to seize the initiative and get the task complete.

83 – Service test

BLUF: As a teacher you need to hold yourself to a high standard than those in society at large.

In the Army, we have something called the service test. This is essentially a way of determining if an individual is upholding what is expected of someone representing the Queen and the country. In teaching, a similar test does not exist but applying some of the military principles of the service test can keep you on the right track as a leader.

The first thing to note is the idea that the service test takes place both when on duty at work and when outside of work. As a teacher, you are in the public eye and your level of professionalism is of the upmost importance. You must be seen to have a strong moral compass. If you cannot commit to these high standards, then a teaching job is not for you, get a 9-5.

The service test covers many of the areas we have already explored:

a) Courage

b) Discipline

c) Respect

d) Integrity

As well as two that have not been explored in this book:

a) Loyalty

b) Selfless commitment

Loyalty in the Army is about binding teams and individuals. In this sense, it works in schools whether within year groups, subject departments, or one of the other areas you can work in as a teacher.

Selfless commitment is an area anyone in the Army or teaching will be familiar with. Everyday in these two professions you put others before yourself.

The other three areas to consider are what the Army refers to as standards:

a) Lawful

b) Acceptable

c) Professional

Professionalism is covered extensively throughout this book. Lawful in the Army comes under a range of difficult areas. In teaching, we are generally talking about safeguarding and how you treat the people you work with. In this sense, acceptable behaviour – this links to the two and encompasses teaching being a vocation rather than just a job.

As a teacher and especially as a leader, you should regularly ask yourself If you are upholding these values and standards in your profession. In this way, you can keep on track and be an example to others.

84 – 7 Questions

BLUF: You must have a planning structure, the 7 questions are at the heart of Army planning.

Few planning procedures have quite the same consequences as the Army. You are literally asking your soldiers to put their life on the line and take the lives of others. As such, military planning is scrupulous (planned with military precision!). It is impossible to plan in the level of detail required without an effective structure. For the Army, that is the 7 questions. This is an essential tool in any person's armoury, and was particularly useful over the COVID-19 period, but also for other things such as organising large open days and developing the curriculum. Below is an example of how the 7 questions can be used for planning, specifically looking at the COVID-19 school reopening.

> "Deep thought is essential in the analysis of any military problem. All the factors bearing on the problem must be considered. No matter what his task, every leader must make a logical appreciation of the problem to decide his plan. Any other approach will result in important factors being overlooked and will lead to false conclusions and an unsound plan…."

Brigadier Mansell – "Serve to Lead"

The 7 questions

(Stage 1 – Situational awareness)

1. **What is the situation and how does it affect me?**

We have had a school shut down since 20 March 2020 and we have now been told to reopen, potentially on 1 June 2020. I need to prepare to reopen.

This is also where you can identify questions you have, where answers have not been provided, and plan where you can get the answer.

2. What have I been told to do and why?

I need to have a safe plan to reopen my school – this was given by my superior, the government. I now need to give my governors and parents an outline of the plan and tell my staff the plan in detail.

You can outline here a most likely course of action and the worst-case scenario course of action. In the COVID-19 scenario, the most likely course of action is that Nursery, Reception, Year 1, and Year 6 reopen on 1 June. The worst course of action is that a child in your school dies of COVID-19 as a result of catching the virus in your school. Therefore, keep asking yourself "is the plan in place robust enough to justify your actions?"

The other consideration here is, has the situation changed? In the case of COVID-19, the situation is constantly changing so this area needs to be revisited. It might be that the situation has changed but the plan is still feasible, or the situation has changed and therefore my plan must change.

Issue a warning order:

> "An 80% plan delivered on time is better than a 100% plan finished late"

At this stage, you can issue a warning order (a brief summary of the plan) to staff and give information to parents, with as much information as you currently have. This allows everyone to start planning for how this will affect them. I.e., for a parent, will I send my child back to school?

3. What effects do I need to achieve and what direction must I give to develop my plan?

What do I need to do to make sure I can reopen? How do I make the school safe under government guidance? Also, what is my own knowledge of the school setting?

What is my main effort? In the case of the COVID-19 reopening, Nursery, Reception, Year 1, and Year 6.

(Stage 2 – Development of the plan)

4. Where can I best accomplish each action or effect?

Here you need to consider where you are going to achieve your plan using the consideration from question two. I.e., a requirement to split classes in half means ensuring you have enough classrooms in viable locations to ensure the children can return. In terms of pick up and drop off at school, how are you going to achieve this and ensure maximum social distancing?

You can also annotate maps and photographs to make your plan understandable. For example, a sketch map of the process for pick up and drop off.

5. What resources do I need to accomplish each action or effect?

This is where you need to decide on the people that you require to make your plan work and the necessary equipment. This includes how many staff to have in place to make the plan safe and achievable whilst having the minimum number in to allow for social distancing. You also need to plan the missions and tasks for each department or individual.

What equipment do you need? We have supplies of PPE and have built a hand wash station for outside each school building. But what else might we need?

6. When and where do the actions take place in relation to each other?

Timing is critical and this where you need to use a synchronisation matrix to plan where everything is taking place in relation to each other. For example, ensuring staggered socially distanced drop off and pick up and ensuring that playtimes do not clash or create issues with movement around the buildings, compromising the health and safety procedures you have in place. This also ensures you have enough equipment and personnel to achieve your plan, in the locations you require them.

7. What control measures do I need to impose?

This is the final question and covers key final health and safety considerations. For example, many children will have taken their medication home. Is there a plan in place to ensure these are brought back to school and checked? If a child is not with their regular teacher, are vital pieces of medical information accessible?

At the end of this process, you will have your plan.

In using the 7 questions, you can plan for every eventuality in the schools in the given scenario. There is a five-step process to approach this with. After the 7 questions and the creation of your plan, you then need to prepare to implement the plan and then issue it to the people who are tasked.

R – Receive (i.e., you receive the order, in the case of COVID-19 school reopening, the guidance from the government)

E – Extract (i.e., you take the relevant information for the order you received. Not all the information in the DfE guidance was relevant to all schools)

E – Estimate (using the 7 questions above)

P – Prepare (i.e., getting everything ready)

I – Issue (i.e., the order and direction for successful completion of your plan)

Many other planning tools exist but, particularly in times of crisis, it is best to use what you know or if you do not have a system, use one!

7 Questions planning grid

1. **What is the situation and how does it affect me?**	What are my capabilities?
2. **What have I been told to do and why?**	What is my superior's intent and what is my part in the plan? What are the specified tasks and what are the implied tasks? What constraints are imposed upon me? Has the situation changed?
3. **What effects do I need to achieve and what direction must I give to develop my plan?**	What effects do I want to achieve? (an effect is something you need to be successful)
4. **Where can I best accomplish each action or effect?**	What is the priority order of my effects and where and how can they best be achieved?

5. **What resources do I need to accomplish each action or effect?**	Allocate people and resources
6. **When and where do the actions take place in relation to each other?**	Co-ordinate all timings, use a timeline
7. **What control measures do I need to impose?**	Communication Emergency procedures

85 – Oodaloop

BLUF: Process the information, plan, and seize the initiative.

The Oodaloop is another key military planning tool. It stands for:

Observe

Orient

Decide

Act

The cycle of this then loops back and begins again. Lots of elements act on the Oodaloop, and although typically very military in approach, it is a useful tool for school leaders.

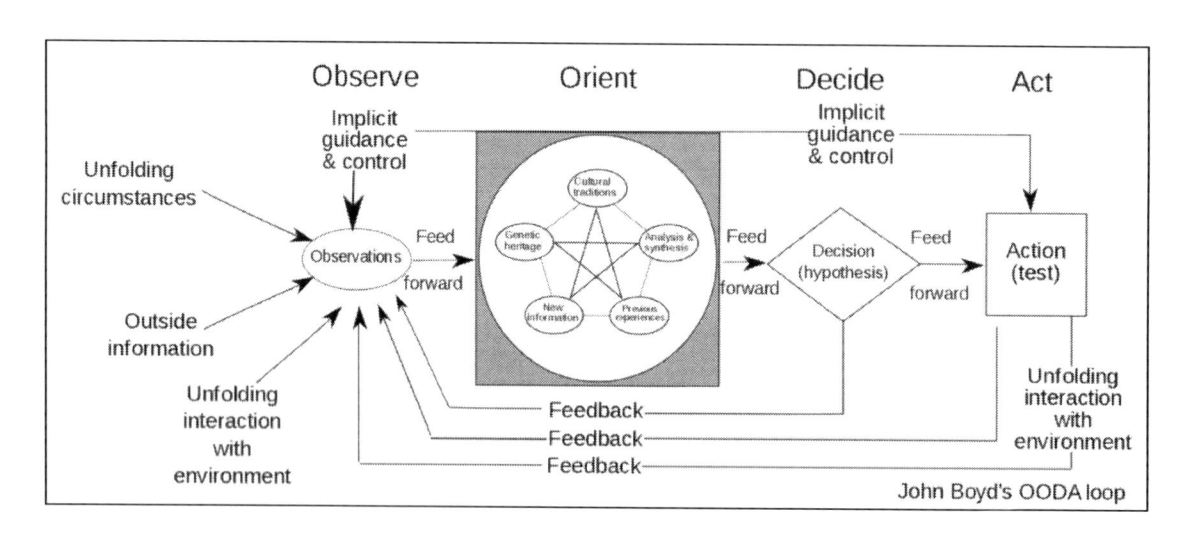

This cycle allows you to process information quickly and react to rapidly evolving events, such as the COVID-19 shutdown. Although the cycle was originally designed to be about defeating the enemy and getting an advantage, quick and effective decision making is essential in education, like any field, at various times. The orient part of the model is often seen as being the most important, as this is when we use our knowledge and experience to shape how we decide to act.

Before that decision is made, you need to observe, i.e., get the relevant information. It is useful to consider the external factors acting on you whilst the cycle is going on, whether that is parents, the government, or your own SLT. This is captured in the feedback stage and allows you to continue building your decision-making profile as you work through the model.

Although the speed of the Oodaloop is often much slower in civilian jobs than the military, where surprise and initiative over the enemy is key, in some instances the speed of decisions and communication of the information can be key to inspiring confidence. In the COVID-19 period, parents wanted to see clear and decisive action from school leaders in and amongst the chaos of the world around them. The Oodaloop allows for rational thinking, whilst others are thinking irrationally and stockpiling toilet paper and rice!

86 - SOPs

BLUF: Have simple procedures in place that everyone can follow.

SOPs or 'standard operating procedures' are at the heart of the British Army. SOPs exist for everything from how to pack your kit, how to march, polish your boots through to conducting a platoon attack. By having SOPs in place, each person has an understanding of how a task should be completed. Although this might sound excessive in a school, introducing SOPs brings understanding at all levels to tasks that otherwise have huge levels of interpretation. SOPs will already exist in most schools for key health and safety areas, such as fire drills, even if they are not called SOPs. Some of the other key areas to employ SOPs are:

a) **Reports** – Reports are a phenomenally time-consuming part of being a teacher. Although most teachers are given a word limit to operate in, without standard SOPs many mistakes will occur leading to inconsistencies across the school, which looks bad to parents. Have SOPs for how many times a child's name should be used in the report or whether to write 'Year 7', 'year 7' or 'Y7'. Standardise whether department names should be capitalised or not, the same for topic names. The list goes on but a couple of pages of SOPs designed to your school will professionalise the process and save everyone time.

b) **Open days** – Open days are one of the more complex events in a school's calendar. SOPs should exist so every classroom and department knows what is expected of them and each individual knows what they are doing.

c) **Assembly entrance and dismissal** – In most schools, this is the largest individual movement of people. Without effective SOPs for entrance and dismissal, the assembly is not only unsafe but chaotic. We have everything from which order classes enter to what pupils should be doing on arrival and dismissal from the hall.

d) **Trips** – Trips are one of the most high-risk areas for a school. You are taking children, often to unfamiliar environments, where a lot of external factors are operating against you. Having SOPs in place, first for the planning of the trip (i.e., letter to parents, money from parents, risk assessment) allows you to get the trip effectively planned and financed before leaving. Having SOPs in place on the trip will minimise risk, this can include what the children should bring on the trip and how to pack it, down to having a buddy system so you do not lose anyone.

At my school, we have short simple SOPs in a vast number of areas, allowing for understanding at all levels and importantly command and control at all levels of the school.

87 - Seek early victories

BLUF: Identify the quick wins and take them.

If leading a school is like turning an oil tanker, one thing all leaders can do at all levels is work for quick wins. This will allow you to stamp your dominance on a situation, department, team, or year group, without being overbearing. One way to get the ball rolling on this is to make sure that you have had an effective hand-over-take-over (HOTO) with your predecessor and meet with all members of your new team. The HOTO process is an essential part of the Army. In some roles, you will spend a week or more shadowing the previous person in post so that you have a full understanding of their role. Although this is more complex in teaching due to time constraints, most schools will accept that you need at least a day in the school before joining, and if taking an internal promotion, you can plan and HOTO, over several weeks.

As a Head, I spent a huge chunk of my first term sitting down one-to-one with every member of staff in the school. Each member of staff was given a fifteen-minute slot.

Prior to the meeting, I had led an INSET session to outline my vision for the school and I asked each member of staff to write down a BHAG (big hair audacious goal) for themselves and the school. This allowed the common ground to be quickly accessed in the meeting and was also very telling on each personality. Some BHAGs were grand, i.e., become a Head, complete a PhD, whereas others were more modest suggesting that they were not BHAG people. The same was true with answers regarding the school, some had grand plans for our development, whereas others were happy with our current state. The other two questions I asked every staff member was:

a) What do you like about school?

b) How could I make your life easier at school?

Of course, I also asked them about their life, family etc and developed conversation from there. The vast majority gave amazing answers about the school. The people to be wary of were the ones with notes books with an extensive list of gripes. Asking how I could make their life easier gave a huge number of quick wins. Although some requests were unrealistic, i.e., no marking, no lunchtime duty, the majority were really simple. For example, "can we get a spare computer upstairs in the office?", "Our coffee machine has been broken for six months, can we get a new one?", "Can the skylight in my room please be finally cleaned?". Within two weeks I had managed to delegate and solve so many of these small problems, giving a quick morale boost and reinforcing that I was someone who listens and crucially, acts.

My other critical early victory, throughout the Army and teaching, has been food. If soldiers are well fed and watered, they are happy. The same is true of teachers. In Afghanistan, I requested that everyone and anyone sent me good ground coffee. We had few luxuries at the time, but good coffee was one of them. Every morning, as is custom, I would arrive in the office thirty minutes or so after my troop Sergeant so he had time to clear up any immediate issues, and then I would brew fresh, good coffee for all of my troop. This became a real bonding experience for us as a group and continued for the length of the tour.

In teaching, cake always goes a long way. In my first middle leadership role as Head of Year 7, I was keen for my office to be seen as the year group's space as well as mine. As such, I started to bring in weekly cake for my team - this brought everyone together to exchange stories and allowed me to take the time to thank the staff for the great work they were doing. Now as Head, I make sure there is cake in both staffrooms every Friday and at the end of each half-term, food and drink is put on for all of the staff to celebrate – again, an opportunity to thank everyone. Early victories!

88 - Leadership is lonely

BLUF: Leadership is a lonely job; it comes with the territory.

Leadership can be a lonely profession. As a younger platoon commander, coming from an environment at Sandhurst where I was surrounded by hundreds of other young officers, joining a platoon can be a shock to the system. You are suddenly supposed to be leading everyone around you and avoid friendships with subordinates. In teaching, the loneliness becomes starker as you progress; from the staffroom banter of being a classroom teacher, to the progressive isolation of being on SLT, to finally being the Head where almost everyone is kept at arm's length.

It can, at times, feel isolating as a school leader. Especially when you join SLT, you are going to be treated differently to when you were less senior. People are often going to be more cautious about what they say about you and many of the casual conversations of the classroom are out of the window.

It is natural to feel the loneliness of leadership, especially in the early months of your appointment. It is difficult, to almost impossible, to be a leader and a good friend to someone. Distance is important as it keeps you neutral and avoids difficult conversations where you have to pull rank on someone you have round to your house for dinner on a Saturday. Perhaps even more important is that you need to allow your staff to bond and that is very unlikely to happen if you are present.

It is important to build strong connections and friendships outside of your workplace to offset the loneliness of leadership. Having a mentor or a coach can also allow you clarity of thought in the lonely world.

89 – Inspection

BLUF: At all levels of your career you will experience this, embrace it.

Inspection is something that you will inevitably experience, whether OFSTED or ISI, inspection is part of the job. Understandably, a level of accountability is needed in schools. Senior leaders should avoid talk of inspection as much as possible to avoid undue stress and to also make sure everything you are doing is not about inspection. There is nothing worse than an answer to a question of why we are doing something being, for inspection.

When inspected, you are given little notice and schools often go into overdrive when the call comes. Ideally, you should be relatively well prepared, but something will ultimately need to be cleared up in the build-up. Lesson observations and interviews will take up the majority of staff time, everyone should clear their diary, whilst appreciating (hopefully) you have nothing to hide. Although inspections are in many respects subjective, overall judgements to some extent are going to be accurate and if they are not, it is the job of the senior leadership to prove it. A truly outstanding school will not be rated as requires improvement (RI) and a RI school is not going to be rated as outstanding. Granted, a good school could end up outstanding and vice-versa without a proper case being put forward by the senior leadership team.

Becoming an inspector yourself, if available, on a part-time basis is great CPD and gives you a clear insight into what is expected in your own context as well as others. Fully understanding the inspection criteria goes without saying and the more staff who know this the better.

You have to be ready to fight your corner. If you do not agree with the judgement you are given, you need to be able to evidence otherwise, if not, you will not have a leg to stand on.

90 - Extreme ownership

BLUF: You are the leader and if it goes wrong, it is your fault.

Jocko Wilink, the former Navy Seal, has written extensively about the theory of extreme ownership and as a leader, it needs to be at the heart of your philosophy and those in your team. The Army, much like teaching, is built around hierarchies. The Army has a very clear rank structure with Generals at the top and command disseminated to subordinates across a range of layers. In schools, you have the Head Teacher, Senior Leaders, Middle Leaders and Teachers. Few schools have broken away from the core model, albeit it many schools now have executive leaders and various other roles in place.

Under the concept of extreme ownership, anything that goes wrong in the school is the Head's fault. They are the ultimate leader of the school and it is their failing if books are not marked in a specific class or someone does not show up for their duty. This might sound ridiculous; a Head cannot be micromanaging every aspect of the school from knowing if books are marked to the quality of every lesson. Under extreme ownership, the Head will instil extreme ownership into every layer of their senior leadership team, and in turn, the senior leadership team into every layer that they lead and so on. The reason the buck stops with the Head is that a single failing in the school is because they (the Head) have not trained or led the person(s) responsible for the individual who has not marked their books properly. This could look like a chain of command as follows – Head – Director of Studies – Head of Department – Teacher. If you have extreme ownership in your organisation, the Head will have instilled that in the Director of Studies who will have instilled extreme ownership in the Head of Department, and the Head of Department in his staff. This creates a culture of owning mistakes and therefore less will happen. Extreme ownership creates a cohesive team that is responsible for its actions. Therefore, someone not marking their books is less likely to happen and if it does, they will take ownership of that mistake.

Of course, not marking books is minor compared to, for example, a child dying on a school trip, which unfortunately does happen. The Head will have signed off on that trip and if the death is a result of an ineffective risk assessment, the Head will be as culpable as the trip leader, even though it may have happened on the other side of the world. In 2003 in the tragic Baha Musa case where the Iraqi civilian was killed by members of the Duke of Lancashire Regiment, the case went to court and soldiers were sentenced with manslaughter and inhuman treatment. Despite not being physically present, the Commanding Officer was charged with negligently performing a duty for his failure to have ensured a situation such as this had occurred. Extreme ownership, responsibility at all levels!

91 - There are no casual conversations

BLUF: As a leader, no conversations are casual.

In teaching, there are no casual conversations when you are the leader, especially when you are the Head. Anything you say can either come back to bite you or be misconstrued by the person hearing it. I realised this in my very first day as Head when I commented on how I was enjoying the music a teacher was playing from their classroom and she turned it off and apologised for the noise, the exact opposite of what I was saying.

How often do you hear someone us the SLTs name or the Heads name in an attempt to give weight to their argument? Well, *the Head said… SLT have said…* This is why you have to be careful about how you communicate. As the leader, you set the example and others will follow. You can ill afford to be a drain rather than a radiator when leading, unless you want to build a toxic culture.

This makes the staffroom a difficult area for senior leaders and is a reason why the SLT often avoid being there. It is a space for staff to decompress and the SLT need to decompress elsewhere, hence the value of a mentor or coach.

Casual words in the corridor with staff about disciplining someone or how poor their lesson is soon becomes wildfire in the school and makes not only the person discussed look foolish, but you.

Avoiding casual conversations as a leader can be difficult because you essentially do not have any downtime. The conversations of leaders motivate and indeed, demotivates people, whilst also changing relationships and trust in the school.

92 - Never say yes in the corridor

BLUF: People will try and catch you off guard, do not commit to something in the corridor.

How many times have you found yourself rushing from your office to a meeting or a lesson and a member of staff just wants one minute of your time? They are about to drop something on you that you are more likely to say yes to because that will get rid of them and allow you to get to where you are going on time. A 'no' answer will invite more discussion and you do not have time for that.

Later, on reflection, you remember that you have committed to something you would never have said yes to in a million years with some proper thought and consideration. This is why you should never say yes in the corridor, in fact, you should rarely say yes in your office. Many decisions need more thinking time than a quick yes or no on the spot. Get into the habit of telling people you will get back to them and they will soon stop asking in the corridor and will be more considerate and thoughtful with their proposals if they do come to your office.

93 - Coaching/mentoring

BLUF: Having a coach or a mentor will help you seek clarity in your decision making and allow you to develop as a leader.

Coaching and mentoring have come to the forefront of leadership development, particularly in teaching over recent years. Coaching is generally seen as being more performance-driven and take place over a period of up to six weeks. It is often used to help an individual leader through a specific period or challenge in the given phase of the school year. Mentoring is seen as being more about the development of the individual and focuses on the individual's leadership as a whole rather than a specific scenario that coaching would deal with.

Coaching and mentoring can be set up in a school to allow leaders at all levels to develop. The relationships in this scenario will have to be built on trust to be effective, with many coaching and mentoring conversations being brutally honest in their approach.

As a senior leader, especially as the Head, having a mentor can be a critical success factor in your first year where you find yourself moving into the position in the school where you can no longer speak to your colleagues for advice and guidance. Networking with other Heads can be an effective way to find a mentor for your first year but lots of companies and especially affiliated bodies, such as the ISA (Independent Schools Association), will provide you with a mentor as part of the membership.

94 - Command and control at all levels

BLUF: Individuals need to have to autonomy to make decisions.

There is nothing worse than being micromanaged. If you have ever worked in an environment where someone micromanages you, it is stifling, and you lose the will to work to the best of your abilities.

In the Army, command and control is actively encouraged at all levels. This means allowing each individual at each level the freedom and authority to make decisions. Rather than the leader of the organisation or the team/department making every decision, each person needs to feel they have the autonomy to affect and shape their environment. By ensuring you have realistic parameters in place you can manage this very effectively in a hierarchical organisation. Individuals need to know what they can and cannot influence. For example, a school will have a whole school marking policy that they are expected to follow but departments will have budgets for their own expenditure rather than having to run every single purchase through the accounts department.

Even on a classroom level, the individual teacher needs to have the autonomy to decide when they are going to mark their books and to a degree, what they are going to teach. By having command and control across all levels of the organisation, it frees the leaders at each level to make fewer decisions but with more time for consideration and fewer decisions fatigue overcoming them. At the same time, it allows everyone the chance to develop their decision-making skills, take extreme ownership and therefore leadership ability whilst feeling in control of their fate.

95 - Slow leadership - condor moment

BLUF: Avoid becoming reactionary in your leadership, sometimes slow is better.

Teaching is a fast-moving environment with hundreds, if not thousands of decisions being made each day. It is easy to fall into the trap of becoming reactionary, responding to every email and decision as it comes in, rather than taking the time to think and defuse the situation.

In the Army, we talk of condor moments. Bizarrely the term condor has its origins in a 1980's tobacco commercial. The person in the commercial meditatively smokes, blocking out the world around them. Although I am not suggesting you start smoking, taking the time to pause and think is essential. In the Army condor, moments are most commonly referred to when under fire. Rather than jumping up as the leader and returning fire on the enemy, you take a moment to pause and think before giving reasonable orders to your soldiers. Taking time to plan your next steps is essential. You need to give yourself headspace. In some instances, this could just be a few seconds or minutes, if you are under fire from the Taliban you won't want to take any longer, or it could be several days in the case of big decisions.

In a time of crisis, in particular, it can be all too easy to jump in with a decision or solution only to discover hours or days later that it was the wrong move, and you should have given it greater consideration. I made this exact mistake during the COVID-19 lockdown, jumping too early telling parents they would have to pay full fees whilst the school was closed, only to backtrack and have to give a substantial discount a week later. Taking a condor moment under pressure allows you to make the right decision and back yourself when the answers and next steps are unclear. This links closely to the idea of slow leadership. Leading a school is often referred to as steering an oil tanker, try and change direction too quickly and the whole ship will capsize. You need to turn the wheel slowly if you are to successfully navigate the choppy waters of a school.

Taking a condor moment, leading slowly not only gives you time but also allows people to build faith in your decisions. No one wants a reactionary leader who's barking out orders on the spot as soon as something happens, it is okay to say you will get back to people. You need to consider the standard that you are going to set. If you react quickly and go back on your word, people will expect you to do this all of the time, reducing your credibility. At the same time, if you reply to every email within an hour, people will come to expect this. Whereas sometimes waiting just a couple of days can see a situation defuse.

Next time you are faced with a difficult decision, take a condor moment.

96 - The standard you walk past is the standard you accept

BLUF: No one is perfect, but you set your own standards and it needs to be high.

True integrity is doing what is right even when no one is watching. The standard you walk past is the standard you accept because if you are not willing to do anything about it, what makes you think anyone else will? This could be little things like picking up a piece of litter in the playground to picking pupils up for poor uniform standards or inadequate work.

At Sandhurst, this is drilled into Officers every day through various training methods including highly polishing your boots, ironing your kit, and ensuring you march everywhere outdoors when on camp (literally marching miles per day, this is how you manage to burn over 6000 calories per day). However, it is best seen through the daily process of areas. The camp is split up into areas that are covered by each platoon in the Academy. For example, each morning, before breakfast, fifteen minutes is spent picking up any litter in your area. I question if there is a cleaner place on Earth than Sandhurst. This daily habit drills in the idea that the standards you walk past are the standards you accept.

You must strive to be the best you can be each day, and in turn, your pupils and the school you are working in. If a culture can be built where everyone or almost everyone believes in this, the pupils will make phenomenal progress. Much of this will take courage and commitment but it will be worth it for the longer-term gains. Things like this cannot happen overnight, but they can happen through years of dedication. At some time, you are going to need your staff or pupils to go the extra mile and having the right habits in place will allow you to successfully do that when the time comes, whether it is an inspection, exams, or some other problem such as COVID-19.

No one is perfect and everyone will make mistakes and their discipline will fall at times. It is about what you are like most of the time, recognising your mistakes, and picking yourself up for next time. In the Army, we often talk about your moral compass and the direction it is facing - north is on track and south is someone who is morally bankrupt. Where do you sit? What standard do you accept?

97 – Get comfortable with being uncomfortable

BLUF: For your own mental health, you need to let things slip so you can sleep at night.

Lots of the best learning in life takes place when you are totally out of your comfort zone. The COVID-19 crisis, as a Head, was my shining moment of leadership glory, but also my darkest hour. The same could be said for my time in Afghanistan. I had the opportunity to truly lead in one of the ultimate leadership areas, war, but I also had to deal with the very dark aspects that come with such an environment.

These uncomfortable areas are where you can truly grow and develop as a leader and often you will look back on difficult experiences and see how your leadership grew, albeit it can be very difficult to see in the heat of battle. The more you have the experiences, the more comfortable you become with being uncomfortable.

When things are going wrong, it can be easy to allow things to spiral and lose all sense of control. In these moments, you must take a condor moment and recalibrate, calling on your team as required for help and guidance, no one needs to do anything alone. That is why schools and the Army have the hierarchy in place that they do.

Do not let your blood boil, it is vital that you can keep a cool head when things are going wrong, this requires mental resilience and must be practised for you to become effective at it.

Finally, never be too proud or embarrassed to admit you are wrong. There is nothing wrong with people seeing that you are human.

98 - The power of habits

BLUF: Habits are hard to break so you need to have the right work management and leadership habits in place.

The majority of what we do is a habit. Habits are very hard to change with the suggestion being that it takes at least five weeks to break a habit. That is why at Sandhurst the new recruits are all put through an intensive first five weeks, to break their old habits and start new ones.

It is too easy to get into the habit of working late or working on the weekend. You need to get habits in place that work for you and your wellbeing. That is why you need to make second nature, your best nature. It is not enough to have one productive day or one day where you get a good night's sleep, this needs to become an everyday thing if you are to thrive as a teacher and a leader.

What stops many people is the idea that they cannot possibly achieve what they need to in less hours than they currently operate. The problem is that if you always use Sunday afternoon to catch up on emails, you will always do that until you make space in your week to achieve this.

A good time to start new habits is always at the start of a new academic year or at the start of a new term. It is worth telling others what you are planning to achieve so that they keep you accountable. If you are planning to leave before a certain time each day, why not tell the person in the office next to you to check-in before they leave. This can be a good way to create artificial pressure to work more efficiently.

By identifying some key areas to improve in, second nature can become your best nature.

99 -Is this the hill you want to die on?

BLUF: You are going to face a lot of issues. Choose which one you will die for.

You get all sorts of characters in schools. There are 480,000 teachers in the UK and schools are supported by a huge number of staff from cleaners and sports coaches to administrators and teaching assistants. The levels of experience can be vast, teachers straight out of university, and teachers who have been in the classroom over thirty years. Levels of education can be anything from minimal GCSEs to doctorates. Schools are a melting pot of emotions and experience.

I see schools as a huge jigsaw, the head has the overall view of the jigsaw and what it looks like. Almost everyone else is controlling a couple of the pieces to make the picture whole. In education, people can become very protective of their jigsaw piece, believing that there is nothing more important in the world, whilst also not fully appreciating the picture. Imagine trying to do a 1000-piece jigsaw but the only person who knows what the finished product looks like (the Head) is trying to coordinate another person to place their piece.

The idea of "is this the hill you want to *die* on" is about choosing your battles. You cannot keep everyone happy all of the time, it is your job as a leader to remain rational in your thinking when others are not. In this sense, the hill is there for you or the staff member to *die* on. Sometimes you will have battles, often over trivial things – you need to decide how big the impact of the yielding ground is and if that is the hill you want to *die* on. At the same time, you can overcome it. It links to the idea that in the Army when faced with a big hill and a heavyweight to carry, you want to get over it rather than *die* on it.

At the same time, it is important for staff to understand this concept because you also do not want to provide the hill for them to die on, you need to get them over the top.

100 – Headship

BLUF – Being a Head is extremely varied and one of the ultimate leadership challenges.

It has been suggested that less than 1% of teachers want to be Heads. So, what puts people off the top job in a school? More than anything, leadership is lonely, being the Head means being generally isolated from every other staff member in the school. Although you can network with peers in other schools, it is very difficult once the Head to have anything more than a clear leader-staff member working relationship. Most teachers join teaching for the joy of developing young minds and being in the classroom. Once a Head, you are, in most cases, totally out of the classroom and rather than leading and developing young minds, you are leading adults - for many, this is diametrically opposed to why they became a teacher. The final key aspect is carrying the weight of the school, the buck stops with you when you are the Head, if it is not working under the principles of extreme ownership, it is your fault.

So why become a Head? It is one of the ultimate leadership challenges and allows those with an interest in leading a wide arena to develop their leadership skills. You have teachers, support staff, pupils, and parents to lead, and that is before you consider other factors such as inspection, local authorities, and government. Few leadership roles have such a diverse role of invested individuals. As the Head, you get to mould the school, gone are the days of wondering what you would do if you were in charge, you are now in charge and you can make all the wonderful things you think makes a great school happen. It allows a level of financial comfort. Many Head jobs come with a six-figure salary, good pensions, and a wide range of extras such as a house, private health insurance and fee discounts (if an independent school).

Most Heads are still referred to as '*the new Head*' until they have done three or four years in post, so choosing the right school is more important than ever. Committing to being Head of a school rarely means less than five years and in many cases far more. All schools have their unique challenges for Heads, and you can find yourself in a single day going through every role from managing finances, leading assemblies, appointing staff, choosing the new colours for the carpets, and having lunch with parents. It is a varied but highly rewarding job.

Conclusion

Most aspects of teaching are not that difficult. What is difficult is tying together the five areas of your personal skills, classroom skills, professional skills, looking after your career and being a leader, all at once, whilst working with, teaching, and interacting with thousands of invested parties.

If you are to succeed in teaching, whether remaining in the classroom for your whole career, or becoming a middle/senior leader, you must get these five areas right. This does not happen overnight. In fact, it usually takes years to get close to and requires years of continuous practice and a commitment to always strive to improve. However, it can be done, and teaching can be a really fulfilling career for you. The variety of roles and positions is vast, and job security is high. Most importantly, it is a rewarding job that will allow you to make a real impact on people's lives. When you are retired and thinking about your legacy, what will it be? If you have spent a career in teaching, that legacy will be young people remembering you and the impact you had on their lives. This could have been teaching them to read, instilling a love of the Tudors, or guiding them to the A Level grade that got them into their dream University, which subsequently shaped their entire life. Few other careers offer this, perhaps the military and the medical profession, but nothing compares to developing people in their most formative years.